Coaching
People
in Sports

Mascot Books
560 Herndon Parkway #120
Herndon, VA 20170

info@mascotbooks.com

PRBVG0115A

ISBN-13: 978-1-63177-036-4

Printed in the United States

www.mascotbooks.com

Coaching
People
in Sports

How to Develop
Successful People and
Exceptional Athletes

Dr. Lee Hancock

Foreword by Jimmy Conrad

Dedications

Some thoughts as I send this book into the world.

To everyone at Mascot books - thanks for the opportunity, and for the quality craftsmanship when preparing and presenting my work. To Jeremy Evans - thanks for cleaning up my writing; perhaps in retrospect I did ok with that first team!

To the many people that read, and gave me advice on, the book; good stuff and thanks.

To the many, many, many teachers, coaches and friends that have impacted me as a person, teacher and coach - I am only able put these ideas out there because of you.

To Jimmy – thanks for the foreword, it's as clever as it is truthful...take that any way you would like.

To Rachel – thanks for being a spouse that understands me as a person...and as a competitor.

To my three sons – Jaden, Gavin, and Owen – two things; 1) remember it is just as important to be a good person as it is to be a good _____ (insert your future profession or goings on here) and 2) this is the last moment of this moment you will ever have, so make the most of it and you!

Table of Contents

Foreword

My Journey and Why this Book, and Lee, Are Right on Target

I was sitting at my locker, somewhat hunched over, with my head in my hands and my eyes fixed on the floor. I had just been told, after twelve years of being a professional athlete, that due to some significant injuries, it was in my best interest to retire from the only thing I had ever done in my whole life: Kicking a ball in a certain direction with other grown men in small shorts.

My soccer career as I had known it, and all of the sacrifices that my loved ones and I made to realize and maintain this dream, was over. And my identity went with it. From the super cool guy you could watch on TV who always exuded total confidence because that's what the job demanded, to an official "has been" that had no idea what he was going to do next.

I was numb.

I cried.

Then I laughed at myself for crying because it was going to end at some point, right? I mean, I've seen *The Lion King*. It's the circle of life. So these tears, they were tears of ridiculousness! How dare I cry about the inevitable!

I cried some more.

The mourning process began immediately and I had to put my arms around my trusted confidants to keep me standing upright from the weight of my overwhelming sense of failure. I hadn't ended my career on a high, as a champion like I always envisioned in my head – being carried off the field by my teammates and fans, the celebratory confetti getting stuck in my hair, bottles and bottles of champagne being sprayed all over me in the locker room, my statue being unveiled outside the stadium, the key to the city from the mayor. Instead, it was abrupt and shockingly unemotional to the machinations of the business of sport.

General Manager: "Okay, Jimmy's gone. How much salary have we now freed up to sign someone new?"

Fan: "Ahh, man, poor Jimmy. That sucks. But he was getting older and the younger guy is probably better than him anyway."

Player: "I'm playing next to who now? Who is going to mark the tallest guy on the other team on corner kicks? And don't say me. (Pause) Sorry, I was texting someone. What are we doing after the game tonight?"

League Office/Sponsors: "Do we have another American defender who can speak in complete sentences that we can market to our fans?"

I became an instant afterthought and so, my choice was made for me. I had to move forward like everyone else, but which way was forward? And what was my destination?

Reflection, Transition and the Point of this Book and Lee's Approach:

As I started out on this new path, I was forced to reflect and rethink who I was and what the hell I was going to do...enter Dr. Lee Hancock.

As I started to chat with Lee, I reflected and processed stuff a bit. Yes, I was pissed off, but we talked about who I was, what I wanted, and how this might be the best thing for me and my family over time.

The injuries I had sustained were head injuries and the discussions with the coaching and medical staff centered around possible next concussions and how those might impact me...my wife...and my kids. None of those discussions had a sensational ending. After a bit of time and some tough discussions, the final decision was one that was looking out for what was best for me as a person, not just an athlete.

And so, on to the point of this book.

As I have reflected on this event (as well as countless other discussions and events in my career) and the thoughts behind the decision that was made for me, some of the best coaches I've had, yes they always knew their stuff, but they also found ways to connect with their players as people. Lee has not just done a great job of giving advice to new and developing coaches, but he also practices what he preaches and uses this approach with people he works with.

Under the steady guidance of Lee, what once looked like a hazy maze of self-doubt and insecurity became a clear A-to-B path to my renaissance. I had a goal and, more importantly, a plan on how to get there. I jumped in with both feet and became something new.

Lee coached me as a person through the harsh reality of knowing that I would have to start over and learn multiple new skill sets, which isn't an easy task for someone like me; someone who'd already been successful at something and wasn't that interested in beginning from the bottom again. Lee nurtured my confidence to a level that could handle the everyday disappointments of not being good enough in my first year post-career. Even now, he brings me back down to earth since my newfound success could be going to my head. Lee has never wavered in his belief that I can have a positive impact on my life and the lives of others.

Lee's almost magical powers of reason and reassurance, while, of course, having careful consideration for my tender ego, was vital to my new iteration, Jimmy 2.0. It helped me develop into the exceptional person I always knew I could become. In fact, I'd like to think that I was a model for this book!

So read this book! And let him have a positive impact on you, too.

Now, if you haven't already skipped this part to see who he dedicated the book to, which better be me, here are two more reasons why you should bow down to listen to Lee:

1. He's a great guy, and I'm not just saying that because he asked me to write this foreword.

2. He's been around, he's seen some things, and my life is better because he's in it.

Make him a part of your life, too.

—Jimmy Conrad
On-Air Talent/Writer/Producer
KICKTV – The biggest soccer
channel on YouTube

Prologue

I have coached since I was 18 years old. The first team I coached was an under-13 boys soccer team, which of course in retrospect is laughable because I was only five years older than the players (and with zero coaching experience and even less teaching experience). When I started with this group I had no idea what I was doing. I knew I enjoyed working with the boys and truly wanted to help them get better, but I had no idea where to start. So, like any young coach, I first reflected on how I was coached, then I watched how other coaches coached, and lastly became educated.

The reflection period was over very quickly. As a youth soccer player I was coached by parent-coaches with little or no coaching background. As a high school athlete, I was coached by twenty-somethings, people who were barely old enough to make quality choices themselves. While both groups were caring folks, I can honestly say I don't remember learning much about the game from them. And, of course, at that time I certainly wasn't collecting coaching ideas because I was busy trying to figure out the game myself.

The next step, however, is where I started my coaching education process. I had inherited the under-13 team from another coach; she was a parent-coach, but one who had a sense of the game.

She ran some fun dribbling, passing and shooting exercises with the boys. I filed those away.

I furthered my education focus by going to fields where I could watch other coaches coach. Over the next few years I would travel to different fields — both locally and elsewhere to watch various exercises, drills and sessions. I took copious amounts of notes on the sessions. The notes I took included the drills they ran, what the players did, where they went, and how points were scored. I became mildly obsessed with finding the next great drill, exercise or session idea; then I turned to magazines and coaching videotapes.

Watching other coaches coach in person was something I continued to do, but when I discovered that one could order magazines and videotapes of some of the world's greatest coaches doing sessions, I was hooked. I ordered video after video from mail order catalogs. When they arrived I would devour them. I viewed them over and over — each time looking at the way the session was set up, how the cones were laid out, how the players moved in the session, what the players did at the end of the session, and so on.

The last part of my education was attending school and earning coaching licenses. When I first enrolled in school, I didn't even think about using it to get better as a coach. At that particular time I was just concerned about showing up for class. It wasn't until much later (which I describe later in the book) that I truly started to use my education to serve my personal goals. Also, during this time I started to get my coaching licenses.

When I was 19, I took my United States Soccer Federation (USSF) D Soccer coaching license course. This license is granted by the USSF, the governing body for soccer in this country, and I remember thinking the instructor was an absolute genius. He had so many sessions at his disposal it was frightening — sessions to teach passing, dribbling, shooting, etc. He had games, too — and these games incorporated fun and all of the stuff needed to play soccer. This was an eye-opening experience.

By the time I was 22, I was well into my collection of exercises and drills. I had notebooks of "stuff." The best part about getting this "stuff" (drills and exercises) was that I would go and practice them as soon as I got them. Like a kid with a new toy, I would use these ideas right away, setting cones and running the exercises and drills in as close a manner as I could to the person from whom I had collected them.

At this point my complete focus was on collecting "content" in order to coach. Collecting sessions was my way of building my base, because at that time, that's what I thought it meant to be a good coach. In retrospect, perhaps, if I had had some better coaching, or if I had been a more applied student as a young person, I would not have taken this approach. But having worked in teacher/coach education I admit I see "content" as being one of the scariest things to a new coach. If you think about it — if you are a new basketball coach and you are asked to teach a group of kids how to shoot you would both have to know how to shoot and have to have some sort of drill to get them organized.

So content is important, but in time I began to realize there was so much more to being a good coach.

As I continued my quest to improve as a coach, I began to understand that, yes, I needed exercises and sessions but it wasn't about having the next best session but rather how those sessions were presented to people. Over the years I still collected sessions. I still took a copious amount of notes, I still watched other coaches, I still became educated, but I started to watch different things.

I started to really watch. I watched how players perceived information from a coach. I watched how a coach would interact with a player or with a group of players. I watched how coaches would manage an athlete who was having a bad day. I watched how the coach would manipulate the session in a small way and which had massive implications on the results on the field. I watched how feedback was delivered — to whom, the frequency, the tone, the — you name it, I watched it. I watched how sessions were planned and how meticulous the criteria were on which the players would be judged. I watched coaches put their arms around players when they weren't doing well, on and on and on, I watched.

I watched how coaches coached other coaches. I watched the bad ones belittle them, put them under pressure, tell them that that was awful and to do it this way. I also watched those same guys just go out and run a session without really telling someone how to run that session. There was no mention from these bad coaches for what things these emerging coaches could do or say to ensure the players received the information or got better and improved as people as a result of the session.

I watched the good ones. I watched these coaches walk their coaches-in-training through sessions on how to give players feedback in a session to ensure they learned. I watched them give advice on ways in which to work with athletes to get them to think and see things differently. I watched them work with these young, emerging coaches on how to work with and teach people.

Now — to be fair I was learning to watch these things given my schooling and coaching background. I got my BA in psychology, my MS in sport psychology and my Ph.D. in curriculum and instruction/ kinesiology. My courses and mentors required me to think rationally and logically about what it was I was looking at and where I wanted to go with it. As a result I was able to learn to think about and ultimately watch coaches coach differently.

I was also fortunate to be around wonderfully educational soccer experiences — some good and some bad. I played college and semi-professional soccer until I was 25, and in my playing experience I interacted and learned valuable lessons from all kinds of players and coaches. I earned all of my USSF coaching licenses, eventually earning my A license, the highest soccer coaching license granted by the USSF.

I have coached soccer at all levels for almost 20 years. I coached club soccer for some of the best clubs and with some of the best (and worst I suppose) coaches from the United States and Europe. I had an assistant coaching role in Major League Soccer where I was able to watch high-level athletes interact with high-level coaches in some very pressure-filled situations. I have also conducted multiple coach education sessions at various levels, including my experiences as a USSF staff member, where I educated emerging coaches who were trying to get their C, B, and A licenses, respectively. In each one of these situations I was able to not only learn from great people but also put some of my thoughts and ideas into action.

After all of these education, coaching and life experiences, I came to a conclusion: You don't coach a sport, you coach a person. As a result of this realization, I now know that coaching is so much more than just running a drill.

Chapter 1

It's About People

There is always this certain something about great coaches that make their practices, games and legends special. Early on in my coaching career I couldn't put my finger on just what that was or how it was, but it was there. Players left the sessions better than when they came in, and when it came to game time, they were always prepared. And when players spoke about these great coaches — whether in person or in the media — it was with respect, appreciation, admiration and sometimes even a bit of trepidation. The most important thing is that these great coaches had many of the same qualities. From youth to professional and from fútbol to football to basketball — they tended to do a lot of the same things, differently of course, but the same.

So why did I start with the idea that great coaching is more than just running a practice? Early on in people's coaching careers there is a great deal of focus on the learning, and the collection of, drills and exercises for practices. In addition, there is usually some focus on ensuring that the beginning coach has some basic coaching methodology that can be used to administer these drills and exercises in practices. The experiences to learn these drills, exercises and methodology come in many forms.

One way coaches get educated is through coach education "programs" such as coaching licenses or online coaching education certificates or programs. These programs provide a great deal of drills and exercises (content) as well as teaching methodology. This is a critical component in the development of a coach and provides a very important foundation for the emerging coach. However, this is only the beginning.

Other ways coaches learn their craft is by watching and being around great coaches. The novice coach, if he or she is lucky, will have an opportunity to be around and learn from great coaches as they coach their athletes. These great coaches have these sensational training exercises that see the players going here and there and trying this or that — likely with a great deal of success as the session continues. This, too, is only the beginning.

As coaches develop, they get out and try these exercises and employ some recently learned methodology. They get their cones set out, get the players ready and there they go. But the exercise never quite looks like it did when the expert did it. To be fair, sometimes the novice doesn't even recognize that it wasn't the same, but if there were an all-knowing observer looking down, the difference in what the players took out of the expert's session vs what they took out of the novice's session would be huge.

But it isn't just the exercise that the great coach is likely doing differently. The session or exercise really is the tip of the iceberg, as it were. There are a litany of things that a great coaches do both on and off the field and before, during and after practices and games. But how can a young, emerging coach know how to properly move people along a continuum that they are learning to move along as well?

The analogy I like to use is that of a cook vs a chef. A cook will take a set of ten ingredients and make a plain cake, and ultimately it may or may not be sweet and tasty. But the chef will take those same ten ingredients and make a luxurious soufflé. The chef has taken those same ten ingredients and blended them together, in the right way for the right amount of time, and then baked them in such a way that when the oven ding goes off it is this sensationally tasty soufflé. "But what the hell, I'm a cook and I swear I did that same ^*%^& thing and yet I got this flat, average cake! Where did I go wrong?" the cook asks himself.

The young coach did everything that he or she saw the great coach do, but where did it all go wrong? The truth is that coaching is so much more than running a drill or exercise or even coaching a game. Yes, the new coach sets it all up the same and perhaps even said the same ten things that he or she heard the experienced coach say, but were they said the same way? Were the players ready to receive the information because they trusted the coach? Were the players managed during the session or in the weeks leading up to that session? Were the players confident during the session in order to execute what the coach asked them to do?

The exercises and methodology are important, but as coaches become experienced and develop into that special something, they understand that it isn't what you coach, it's how you coach it. That is to say, the many exercises and drills that coaches get and use as part of their daily doings are important, but ensuring players receive this information and are able to use it is another thing entirely. Great coaches are ones that connect with and understand their players to ensure they are learning what needs to be learned so that they can perform when it counts.

Great Coaches Coach People

Great coaches coach people, they don't just coach athletes. Great coaches understand that their players are people and that these people are the ones who are coming to their practices, games, meetings and teams. This basic premise sets the stage for how a great coach organizes and teaches his or her sessions, manages his or her players on and off the field, and in essence runs his or her team.

The great coach understands that athletes don't show up to practices or games as empty vessels; they come with experiences, contexts, stories and backgrounds. They come in as a person, not just an athlete. Teams are made up of individuals and those individuals are all different and need different things every day. Knowing about that athlete as a person, what he or she feels, what his or her goals are or how he or she may need to be motivated, or how he or she needs to think differently about a problem in a practice or a game — necessitates a different starting point in order to understand that person and what he or she needs. The great coach approaches his or her sessions with a different starting point in mind. They coach the person within the sport as opposed to just the athlete. But how do they do that?

A quick look at some of the more well-known managers, professional and college coaches, and perhaps some local youth coaches, may give us some insight into what perhaps a good coach may be doing both on and off the field, and how he or she may be doing it. Let's take a peek at some of these coaches below. As you read the items I urge you to gather more information on these people on Google. During your research you will get an even better picture than I hope to paint.

Jose Mourinho

Jose Mourinho is a well-known soccer figure who has managed some of the biggest clubs in Europe, including Chelsea, Inter Milan and Real Madrid. In his stints at these clubs, he has won multiple championships, including domestic titles, League tournament titles and

European Cups. His teams play very similarly — they are notoriously well-disciplined, tactically organized, and are always competitive. So what is it about his methods that make his teams great?

Let's first look at the content and presentation of his content. It has been said Jose Mourinho uses approximately 40 drills or exercises when he coaches his teams. The details that he puts into the creation and implementation of these exercises are things that set him apart. The exercises are established and then it is said that he meticulously ensures that all players understand their roles within the exercise and then, of course, how that exercise relates to the game. But of course this isn't all that makes him successful, so what else?

Jose's presence and player management is legendary. One of the things that make him a great coach is that he has a presence. Many would call him arrogant, but in all likelihood almost all of those people haven't played for him. What you can ascertain from watching and reading about him is that he carries himself with confidence and comfort, in every situation, no matter how big the occasion. This presence seems to transmit to his players. Many high-profile players talk about him with reverence and indicate how important a figure he was to them…as people.

Sweden's Zlatan Ibrahimović, an extremely talented (and some would say temperamental) soccer player, said this in his autobiography: "Jose Mourinho is a big star…He's nice. The first time he met my partner Helena, he whispered to her: 'Helena, you have only one mission: Feed Zlatan, let him sleep, keep him happy.' That guy says whatever he wants. I like him. He's the leader of his army. But he cares, too. He would text me all the time at Inter, wondering how I was doing." Zlatan continued to gush about Mourinho, his presence and his care for not only the player but the person.[1]

Didier Drogba, another extremely talented soccer player who played for Mourinho, also has this to say about Mourinho. In an interview with *The Daily Telegraph*[2], April 12, 2013, he describes Mourinho and his first interactions with him "I first saw Jose at a Porto-Marseille game six or seven months before that. In the tunnel, he slapped me on the back and said: 'Do you have some brothers who play like you?' Didier goes on to describe his days at Chelsea. "People didn't see Chelsea as a family..." You cannot achieve what we did without being together...Jose is good at developing people. With a player like Eden Hazard, if he listens to Jose, if he eats, and learns what Jose teaches him, he can be really, really good."

You can see from these quotes from these players that Jose was doing much more than just presenting content and running a few exercises. Yes, Jose has his detractors and, of course, some blemishes on his record. But if you look at some of the high praise that players bestow on him, it is incredible. Clearly, Jose is into much more than simply running an exercise or 2v2. He is managing people, through his feedback and presence — he is coaching the person, not the sport.

Phil Jackson

Let's switch sports to basketball and the legendary Phil Jackson. Phil Jackson is a wildly successful basketball coach. He led the Chicago Bulls to six titles over the course of nine years and then he led the Los Angeles Lakers to five titles over the course of ten years. In case you aren't counting, that is eleven titles in less than twenty years — a truly incredible accomplishment. Of course, he had some incredible players, but he also had some incredible content.

Phil Jackson refined and utilized what is commonly known as the triangle offense. When Phil Jackson arrived in Chicago he hired a gentleman named Tex Winter. Tex Winter was previously a head coach at Kansas State University where he utilized and refined his content and presentation of content. Together these two coaches laid out simple, yet complex, exercises and sessions that taught already good players a system that helped them win, and win, and win. Now, some would say it was the system that made the players while others would argue the players made the system — both could be true. I would argue that it was Phil Jackson (and of course his assistants) who ensured that they drove home the content through quality feedback and management of people.

Of course equally as well known as the triangle offense to those that pay attention to sport is how well Phil Jackson was said to have managed and motivated his athletes. When Jackson took over the Bulls he had a young superstar named Michael Jordan who, at the time, hadn't accomplished anything, yet was being relied upon as if he had. So it was said that Jackson borrowed a phrase from a book he had read from an American Buddhist nun. The phrase was: "No man is an island. No man goes his way alone. What I put into the lives of others will come back into its own." It was said that Jackson repeated this statement frequently, thus showing the superstar that he had others' backs (and saying to the others that they needed to have his). Jackson continued to ask Jordan to be part of the team and rely on them as he would himself.

Jordan for his part appeared to accept these requests and in time seemed to appreciate Jackson for so much more than just a guy with content. In an article for *ESPN the Magazine*, Jordan said "Phil is fantastic at managing egos and personalities, getting everyone on the same page and maxing out whatever potential is there for what should be the common and ultimate goal.[3]" With this article it seems that Jordan seemed to understand that Jackson was interested in the person and all that they could get out of themselves, as well as give back to the team. He appears to understand that Jackson was trying to improve the person and challenge them to go beyond and get out of their comfort zones.

Again I am not here to suggest that everything Phil Jackson did was perfect, or that he doesn't have any blemishes on his record, but I will argue that he was so much more than content. And that so much more includes unique ways to communicate, manage players and have a presence all leading to the improvement of the person and player.

Greg Vanney

Greg is a former Major League Soccer, Ligue 1 (French 1st division) and U.S. Men's National Team player and current head coach of Toronto FC in Major League Soccer. Greg has developed elite players at every level in the United States including at the youth, college, professional and U.S. National Team levels. Greg is well-known for his technical and tactical expertise in soccer, but what many people don't know about Greg is his desire and ability to develop the whole person, not just the soccer player.

Greg Vanney does all of the things he does with an eye to developing the whole player. Yes, Greg is world class in his content; his exercises in training, his in-game management and his overall ability to teach the game of soccer. But Greg also puts programs and ideas in place that ensure players are developing in other areas of the game. Greg uses analytics to ensure players' physical workloads are managed. He, and his head of sport science, do this in order that players stay healthy, injury-free and ready to play. This is a very powerful tool as it shows the athlete, through actual data, that you aren't grinding them into the ground but that you are looking out for them and their welfare.

Greg also ensures his players are developing cognitively. Greg, because of his education as a player and a coach, understands that soccer is a thinking game. As a result Greg and his staff create unique opportunities for players to develop critical thinking skills in order that they may be successful, both on and off the field. These thinking skills provide the players with unique opportunities to develop skills that they can use in games and ultimately off of the field as well.

In addition, because Greg places such a high importance on this cognitive aspect, he hired a specialist to manage and properly deal with head injuries. Head injuries are a hot topic in sport and many sports are dealing with the proper way to handle players with head injuries. Greg, because this is important to him, took a very unique step and hired this specialist to not only deal with head injuries but also to manage the players' safe return to the playing field and life. Greg did this, sure because of the impact on performance, but more so because it was the right thing to do for the athlete.

Hopefully as you read about Greg what comes out is that, yes, he is a very capable coach, but more than anything, Greg is a great person. I have been fortunate to be on staff in a professional environment with Greg, and as a result I have seen this firsthand. I have seen many occasions where Greg pulled guys aside and had a chat with them about, yes the game, but also about life and perhaps what that person was going through off of the field. I have seen him spend countless hours working with players, both on and off the field, in order that the player develop in his entirety. Greg knows his content backward and forward, but more importantly Greg knows, understands and cares about people.

Pat Summitt

I must admit I don't religiously follow women's college basketball, but I do follow exceptional coaches, and Pat Summitt is near the top of that list. Pat Summit is the undisputed pioneer of women's college basketball. Ms. Summitt began her 38-year coaching career in 1974. During that time she started programs, won NCAA titles, won Olympic gold medals and, more importantly, championed women's sports and the athletes who progressed through her program. A quick Google search yields story after story about Pat Summitt and her legendary status. While I cannot do her justice in such a small area, I want to lay out a few highlights of her coaching ability that are germane to my argument.

Pat Summitt could flat out coach. By all accounts her "content" and exercises and game management were similar to what was being used at the time, nothing flashy. It was said that she put her own twist on a system that was utilized by the Chicago Bulls in order to win the Lady Vols' first national championship. It was also said that she was also an exceptional "game coach" — making the proper adjustments and tweaks to provide her athletes every opportunity to be successful. But of course, this isn't why so many people say Pat Summitt was great. Many people say that it was the way in which she presented her content and the way she managed the athletes that led to her greatness.

Pat Summitt was said to have demanded accountability relative to her "content." One of the hallmarks of Pat Summitt was that she would set goals with and for her players to ensure the techniques/tactics in the sessions, games and year were accomplished. It was said that she would then hold players accountable to these goals that they had decided on as they moved through the days, weeks and months. But it wasn't the content or the attention to detail in the content, it was the way in which she went about this process that made Pat so special.

Pat created what she called the "Definite Dozen." These dozen items were Pat's coaching philosophy. But no coaching philosophy works unless it is lived and implemented over and over and over. And, based on the number of people and champions she developed, it appears that it was it was lived and done over and over.

Pat Summitt, by all accounts, was an ethical, passionate, demanding teacher of people who happened to play basketball. When asked about her accomplishments, she would frequently remind people that she hadn't made one basket or completed one pass on the way to all of those championships — her players did. If you look at her dozen items they are all items that one would need to be good at basketball and life (e.g., take full responsibility, make hard work your passion, make winning an attitude, etc.). When Pat coached during all of those years, it appears that she ensured the content got taught by ensuring the people learning the content were motivated, managed and provided feedback. She seemed to demand accountability from the person — both on and off the court to the tune of sixteen national titles and a 100 percent graduation record.

I could continue, but for those of you that want to know more I would suggest that you should read the many books written about, or by, Pat Summitt. But for my argument's sake you can see that, yes, she knew the game, but it was her desire to coach the person instead of just the athlete that made her great. She knew her content but more importantly she was able to present it in unique and special ways.

Youth Coaches

At this point many of you might be thinking, okay, these are all pro and college coaches, why not include some youth coaches, or are youth coaches different? I absolutely believe that the same items that make a pro or college coach successful make a youth coach successful. Perhaps there is greater (or less) emphasis on certain components but the essence of that person and the way they handle themselves and situations remains the same. I have chosen to use specific pro and college coaches because information about them is readily available and the reader can get a good picture of what I am driving at. But, as I said, I would argue that good youth coaches do some of the exact same things but with a greater emphasis in some areas than others.

Think about some of the best youth coaches out there (my guess is that you could probably go and Google some of these people as well if you wanted to, or go watch them in person). My point is, if you walked into a great high school basketball coach's office, tracked a quality youth club soccer coach for six months or a year, or watched an experienced hockey coach, you would see them doing many of the same things that the professionals have done, only with children. Many of the same nuances, progressions and ideas but fantastically tweaked to ensure young athletes developed as athletes and people.

Or even more importantly, if you asked some ex-players about that great coach you would hear some of the exact same things that were said about the great ones. You would likely hear about how much that coach cared about his/her team, how they taught life lessons, how they demanded from their players, and likely how they created an environment of expectations and excellence. Sure, you would likely hear about some quality Xs and Os and how they had really good exercises or drills and had some innovative tactical approaches. But my contention is that the players, in time, would likely remember very little about the Xs and Os (the content) but loads about how that coach improved them as an athlete and as a person.

I have seen and worked with many of these great youth coaches, and as a result, have a lot of great examples. One coach I worked with coached boys' high school athletes. This particular coach was fantastic at exercises and drills with his athletes but what made him special was the amount of time he would spend setting goals with his players. He would create a schedule and meet with these players after or before practice (or school) and help them understand what they were after in their sport experience. These goals were many times way beyond just sports, they were about life and what the young athletes wanted to accomplish as young men.

Another coach I worked with was a girl's high school volleyball coach. The student-athletes he worked with were from the inner city and as a result faced unique challenges. This coach worked with these young women to develop them as leaders. Taking time to mentor each of them and working with them on how they could lead not only their teammates, but also themselves, their families, and their peers outside of sport.

The truth is that great coaching is so much more than running a drill or exercise and is absolutely about coaching the person. When you are coaching the person what you are doing is establishing, cultivating and nurturing a relationship.

It's About People, It's About Relationships

A look at the examples of great coaches above, as well as those that you might be able to come up with who also take this approach, show that being a coach that coaches people instead of just athletes is about understanding, developing and nurturing relationships. These relationships establish a basic foundation for a coach to work with these people in their sport. This basic foundation then establishes a starting point for how, when and why a great coach does what he or she does with his or her athletes to ensure success.

But relationships in sports aren't normal "relationships," they are about the coach, the player and those that surround the player, working together in order to improve and learn and ultimately perform. In order to establish relationships and a way to work with people in sport, one must do certain things and adopt certain approaches to how they teach their sport. So how does one establish and cultivate relationships in sport where learning and performance are expected? More importantly, can we determine what these things are in order for new and emerging coaches to use these things with their athletes?

First let's look at just what a relationship might entail. There are various definitions of "relationship" depending on what source you are using. Webster defines a relationship as "…the way in which two or more people, groups, countries, etc., talk to, behave toward, and deal with each other" and "…the way in which two or more people or things are connected." If you think about it, this is the essence of sport.

Sport, as I said above, is a different place to have a relationship — to "deal with each other" and "stay connected." In sport there are expectations of learning and improving and performing. There are expectations on both sides of the fence. That is to say, as athletes move through their sport experience they will want to enjoy their sport experience, learn, improve and perform. The coach will have expectations as well. He or she will expect that his or her players come prepared to work hard, learn, develop, become a part of the team, and in the end perform.

So what things do great coaches do to establish and utilize these relationships as a starting place as they coach their athletes? Well, per the definition of a relationship (and taking into account some of the examples used above) they must do things to ensure that these people and these athletes *work together, deal with each other* and stay *connected* as they pursue their sport experience. They listen to them, talk with them and work with them. They create a place that these people will grow and thrive. They work with them on and off the field in various situations. They make it a *we* thing vs just a *them* thing and they treat these people as people who are working together to get to a certain place. That *place* being improvement, higher performance, the attainment of athletic and life goals, and in some cases, money and or championships.

It's About a Basic Approach to Coaching

The focus on the person and that relationship that connects and ultimately drives these people and pushes them toward common goals is a basic starting point for how a coach might go about coaching their athletes. It is of course about what the coach teaches (their content) and the methodology that they use. But, having a starting place that understands that it is about people, those relationships in sport and how those relationships are created, nurtured and utilized in order to ensure improvement, is the key to high performance in sport.

If we look at all of these great coaches, there are patterns and categories that begin to emerge as they develop their athletes. That is to say the great ones all do certain things or have certain qualities that allow them to coach people instead of just athletes and, as a result, get the most out of those people, not only as people but also as athletes. These categories, these elements, that make up these coaches and their approach, are touchable and tangible things and can be learned.

Chapter 2

The 4 Elements

Great coaches have and use 4 critical elements as they work with their players as people: *presence, environment, management* and *communication.* As previously stated, many young or inexperienced coaches have awesome exercises and "content." The great ones not only have fantastic sessions and systems but also connect with their players, motivate their players, manage their players and overall do truly unique things with their players. In order to ensure the content of the sport is taught and implemented, great coaches create a *great environment* for athletes by having a meaningful *presence, managing situations and people* and *communicating* appropriately. And, of course, the great ones must continually gain experience and improve in order to be great at the 4 elements above.

In this book I set forth and explain these elements as well as the content and experiences that great coaches have and use as they approach their players. The method for how these 4 elements play out for a great coach is a simple formula, which is odd because I am probably the worst person at math that you can possibly imagine. The formula is: **The 4 elements + Content + Experience(s) = a coach.** The 4 elements being *presence* (ones appearance/being/aura), the *environment* (the physical and mental area that exists around and for the athlete), *management* (how/when one manages people and situations), *communication* (how/when one communicates to people): plus the *content,* which refers to what it is one wants to coach and how one wants to coach it, and lastly *experience,* which refers to how a coach develops, as well as what one does to develop as a person throughout life.

This formula is known as "the 4 elements method of coach education." This is a unique way for coaches to think about how they approach, implement, and work with their players as people in sport. I would suggest that this way can be *the* way that a coach educates him or herself to work with their players. Or this book can perhaps be "in addition to" some of the traditional ways coaches are educated in their sport, namely through licenses and coach education programs.

The 4 elements, as well as the content and experience components, are a method I arrived at over time and with a lot of research and deliberate attention paid to great coaches, what they did and how they did it. It is a culmination of years of personal education (being around great people, reading books and articles, etc.), classic education, practical experiences I have had as a student/player with some of the greatest teachers and coaches around, and as a result of creating and conducting multiple teacher and coach education programs from scratch.

I have tried to take all of the best things I have gleaned from each of these experiences and put them into categories (the 4 elements) to help people teach people in their sport. Actually settling on these elements that made up these types of great coaches was a process and is something I would encourage anyone to do too if you are lucky enough to watch great coaches coach. I started with the deconstruction of great coaches. As I started to watch great coaches coach (and in essence deconstruct their doings) I noticed a surprising amount of similarities — in phrases, terminology, philosophy, actions and, of course, the attention paid to the person, not just the athlete.

Once deconstructed the next step was to construct. That is to say, once I had seen what these great coaches did, and of course once I had some experience(s) out and about as a teacher to put what they did in the proper context, I started to put together what I had seen. The construction of this was then: 1) write down what it was they do/did and eventually, 2) put these "notes" into an organized, touchable/tangible format so other people could learn how to do this, too.

Over time these "notes" eventually took the form of the 4 elements. I found that I could take any note on any coach (that wasn't content or presentation of content) and place them into one of the elements, namely presence, environment, management and communication. More importantly though is that once I took those notes and placed everyday things that these people were doing into categories, I found that when instructed, others could learn to do these things as well.

Over the past 15 or so years I have done multiple coach and teacher education projects — some large, some small. Many times I have come into existing places that had great curricula but were lacking something. Moreover, I have continued to coach teams and as a result I am also my own guinea pig when it comes to learning. Am I doing this right? Am I getting better or getting worse as a coach as I use these elements (to be fair sometimes the latter…which has been equally good for my development and the development of this method)? How am I getting here? I have received very positive feedback from groups that I have worked with on these 4 elements — how the 4 elements have helped them improve and ultimately helped their players improve. In addition, I have run this method past coaches and teachers that I massively respect and, thanks to their usage and eventual feedback, this has passed that test as well.

It is my hope that, as you read this book, you truly enjoy thinking about what makes these great coaches great and how you might be able to do the same as you coach your people, who are also athletes. As we establish these 4 elements we will then get into that all-important content and teaching content sections. But at present, on to presence.

Chapter 3

Presence

Reflect back to your favorite teacher or coach, and take a moment to try to remember just what exactly occurred with that person, in that classroom or sport experience, that caused it/them to be a favorite? Do you remember lessons or daily assignments? Do you remember how much you learned or how hard you studied or practiced? Probably to some extent yes, but what you likely remember is how much you appreciated that mentor, how they opened your mind a bit, how they challenged you, made you want to compete against yourself and others, and ultimately, how they made you feel.

But how did they do that? How did they capture your attention, hold your attention and "make" you learn? What was it about them, who they were, and how they were that made them a great coach? If you have ever been around or seen that great teacher or coach you understand that there is just this something about them that captures your attention and imagination.

"Je ne sais quoi" is a French phrase that can be used to describe this type of person. The phrase in French literally means that person has that

"I don't know what" quality about them. In English it is frequently used to describe a person with presence by saying that they have an "indefinable quality" or "that certain something" or that "personality" that makes them unique.

Is it possible that certain something is real or simply an "I don't know what" quality? Is it an identifiable something in sensational coaches? And more importantly, is it replicable and teachable to new and emerging coaches?

Great coaches do seem to have a magical presence. That certain something that, along with their ability to create a great environment, manage and communicate with people and deliver on the Xs and Os, is alive and well and is literally a game changer. Youth coaches have it, college coaches have it, and of course, so do well-known professional coaches.

Sir Alex Ferguson appears to have that certain something; he had, and continues to have, presence. Sir Alex Ferguson was the manager (coach) for Manchester United, one of the most successful teams in the world. Sir Alex managed United from 1986 to 2013. His teams won 49 trophies, including 13 English Premier League titles and the prestigious UEFA Champions League twice. He is widely considered to be one of the most, if not the most, successful soccer managers in history, not only English history, but in the history of soccer.

His content and teaching of content were said to be very impressive as he was considered a very capable tactician in games. Many a game was won because he appeared to make the right choice at the right time to win critical games. Once of the most famous examples of this was in the 1999 UEFA Champions League final when Sir Alex subbed on a young Ole Gunnar Solskjaer, who promptly scored the tying and winning goals in the waning seconds of the game. But Sir Alex is probably best known for his presence, who he was. And it was this presence that many claim was the key to his unparalleled success.

Sir Alex was said to have a presence that was larger than life. Much has been made in the English press about his influence on English national team player selections, game dates and times and of course referees where conspiracy theories abounded as to why so much extra time was always left on the clock when United were losing. (Fergie time!) In addition, there are countless stories about his influence on players (Ryan Giggs, David Beckham, Paul Scholes, etc.); their careers, habits and lives both on and off the field. In fact his presence will forever be felt at Old Trafford (the stadium where United play,) as there is a section of the stands named after Sir Alex — now that's presence!

Yes there were times that his "who he was" appeared to get the better of him. It was said of Sir Alex that he had a bit of a temper; this temper specifically was said to come out at halftimes of certain matches when his teams were underperforming. These rants were sometimes called "the hairdryer treatment." But were these times where he was actually using losing focus or just using his "presence" to make an impact on his athletes?

In his autobiography Sir Alex indicates that his temper served him (and his presence) as he wanted it to and when he wanted it to. Sir Alex indicates that his temper was "a useful tool…It helped to assert my authority. It told the players and staff I was not to be messed about." This isn't to suggest that Sir Alex was never calm, as in his autobiography he also writes that "you're better just calming people down" (when referring to some game and life situations). It appears then that Sir Alex was using his presence in different ways and at different times — perhaps depending on what the situation called for at the time.[4]

When speaking to the Harvard University Business School he provided some unique insight into who he was as a person and how that impacted his staff, his players and his team.[5] Sir Alex said, "Everything we did was about maintaining the standards we had set as a football club — this applied to all my team building and all my team preparation, motivational talks, and tactical talks," he said. "For example, we never allowed a bad training session. What you see in training manifests itself on the game field. So every training session was about quality. We didn't allow a lack of focus. It was about intensity, concentration, speed — a high level of performance. That, we hoped, made our players improve with each session. I had to lift players' expectations. They should never give in. I said that to them all the time: 'If you give in once, you'll give in twice.' And the work ethic and energy I had seemed to spread throughout the club. I used to be the first to arrive in the morning. In my later years, a lot of my staff members would already be there when I got in at 7 AM. I think they understood why I came in early, they knew there was a job to be done. There was a feeling that 'if he can do it, then I can do it.'"

Sir Alex seemed to have had a presence about him that made others believe and want to listen to what he had to say. This is certainly an extreme example of presence but hopefully what comes out in this look at one of the great ones is that presence is critical in great coaches. I do believe that good youth coaches also possess a certain presence. While some of the things in a youth coach are different, the truth is that they also possess that certain confidence or poise that indicates to the athlete that what I say is worth listening to and doing and will help you be successful. The question is, are these great youth, college or pro coaches born with this presence or can it be learned?

I would of course argue that it can be learned. Presence isn't fake, contrived or forced. Now having said that, while you are on your way to having presence, you will probably have to fake, contrive and even force it as you are getting out of your comfort zone. Gaining presence, that poise and confidence, takes time to obtain (likely years in fact, but I will tackle this notion of experience(s) at great length later in the book). But, as of now, the truth is that presence is comprised of certain ingredients that, when combined and baked, over time, can lead to something special.

Presence – The following items are what I have found make up and can lead to one obtaining presence. I have used these with great success to develop teachers and coaches. Again, this is likely not a complete list but I would argue that if you start with these you will be well on your way to establishing and earning the right to have presence.

1. What can we learn from great actors about presence?

If anyone has ever been to a play (and to a lesser extent a movie) and seen a great actor on stage you will likely recall how you felt after watching that person perform. Great actors ensure that whatever role they are playing that you the audience believe that the character they are playing and the emotions that they are displaying are as real as possible. Moreover, if they are truly good at their craft they actually move you to feel for that character the emotions that they want you to feel.

The other thing about actors is that they suspend their own reality when they are playing this character. That is to say, yes, they are remembering their lines and they know where they are but they can take on the persona of that character and deliver the performance, all while still being that other person. The trick is to get enough into character to be that person but still maintain yourself in order to maintain composure so that you recall lines and move about the stage or set to ensure the script.

Great actors have great presence and that presence comes out in various ways. Great coaches have great presence that needs to be developed in a similar fashion to that of an actor. The suggestions below are how many a great coach has, and can develop, his or her presence similar to how an actor might.

Suspend Reality

Getting up in front of people and being a big personality is not easy for some people given that perhaps they are normally a quiet person. Unfortunately, if you want to have presence you must sometimes "own the room" and it'll take you stepping out of that quiet body of yours to ensure this happens. To do this many of these quieter folks simply must "suspend reality" and get into that place that allows them to deliver that speech or item of feedback that is out of their wheelhouse. To be fair it could also be that overly boisterous person that is feeling overwhelming emotion that needs to calm down and ensure his group hears and gets what they need to get.

The point is that there will be times that you may not be feeling something but you know your group needs to feel some emotion. This means you will need to step out of that comfort zone and "suspend your own reality" while delivering the feedback needed for them to be successful. Suspending that momentary reality and stepping out of that comfort zone takes time, but as you do it and self-reflect, you will see that it really does add to your presence and ability to move people along.

The Appearance of An Emotion All While Being Cool and Collected

As I said above, there will be times that you need to get to your group or an individual with a boisterous delivery of information, or on the flip side, a calming diatribe about this or that (when inside you are as focused as ever). Having presence and showing emotion as part of that presence is a key part of some coaches' arsenal. But for one to truly have presence, one will need to be able to switch that emotion very quickly should a player need him or her for assistance during a practice or a game.

Feigning emotion to move a group along sometimes needs to be done. As a leader you always needs to ensure that you can think and make choices, because if you can't, who will? A way to check yourself as you are improving in this area is to self-reflect as you are delivering this type of emotion building. Or, just after you deliver information, can you switch to someone asking you a question or are you still fixated on what you just said?

Reading People's Emotions

Truly great stage actors feed off of the crowd and how they are reacting — guiding people along to ensure they get to where they are supposed to be, when they are supposed to. Sometimes as a coach, as you are delivering information, you need to be able to check on how someone is receiving the information in order that they apply it when you need them to apply it. Great coaches with presence are constantly looking for how their players are receiving the information and emotions that they are setting forth.

One could argue that actors are faking something and that's not good, as we want coaches to be genuine. That is not what I am trying to say. What I am trying to say is that when you are a novice teacher things like getting up in front of people, remembering your session, helping kids learn, managing other things going on around is not easy. But the fact is that when you are in charge of moving people along in a sporting environment you are on stage. And being on stage requires a certain amount of presence; and presence is gained through many a time on stage but also by paying attention to the right things.

I have seen great coaches and they do all of these things that great actors do — with the goal of moving someone along in his or her sport experience. The funny thing is that when I have interacted with a lot of these larger-than-life people they are actually nothing like their on-court/field persona. So, take these ideas and try them and see how they work.

2. Getting and Using Your Voice

Great coaches have a voice that lends to their presence. Coach Lombardi was the head coach of multiple professional football teams. He is most well-known for coaching the Green Bay Packers and coaching them to the first two Super Bowl Championships in the history of the NFL. Coach Lombardi is synonymous with the NFL, so much so that the Super Bowl Trophy is named after him. He is an icon. More germane here, though, is that his voice is synonymous with the NFL.

Flip on any show that talks about the history of the league and you will likely hear his voice bellowing from the sidelines or someone quoting his many famous lines. When Coach Lombardi spoke, people listened. His players listened and the media listened, and he made an impact on everyone around him with his voice and what he did with that voice. Some of his more recognizable phrases include:

- "Winning is not a sometime thing, it is an all the time thing. You don't do things right once in a while, you do them right all the time."

- "Perfection is not attainable. But if we chase perfection, we can catch excellence."

- "There's only one way to succeed in anything, and that is to give it everything. I do, and I demand that my players do."

By almost all accounts, Coach Lombardi was a fierce competitor who created an environment of excellence by who he was and what he did and said. His voice seemed to convey trust and at the same time said "I know what I am talking about and if you listen to me you will get a lot out of this activity, drill or game." Picking through those quotes it is clear that he used his voice to convey information in a way that was demanding but also motivating and informative at the same time.

How many times have we seen veteran, well-known coaches and their speeches replayed on television? Many times those speeches are loud and aggressive speeches meant to rile up the team and get them prepared for battle. But that's just a small way that a coach uses his or her voice to ensure presence. What about the time that a player is messing around and the coach simply says in a calm voice, that is unacceptable behavior and we don't behave that way here, do we? The veteran coach's voice clearly indicates that he or she is in control, knows what he or she is talking about, and the words that come out are to be listened to and followed.

Young, inexperienced coaches by contrast have a voice that is timid, unsure and somewhat on point vs absolutely on point. Young coaches think they know what to say as opposed to the veteran coach who knows what to say and when to say it. They are searching for what to say and when to say it relative to what it is they are trying to coach.

Voice refers to one's teaching voice and how and when a coach uses that voice. Voice doesn't refer to being overly loud and powerful with one's sound. A coach's voice can be soft, loud, empathetic, stinging, loving, but it must be well-timed, well-thought out and ensures there is a response as a result of what he or she says. This voice is a key component to a coach's presence and something that can be developed over time, and in many ways, to ensure that their players are receiving their message.

Following are a few key ways that one can think about, use or get their voice. Certainly there many more ways but these are a good start.

Getting Your Voice

The majority of good singers think they are good singers because they sing in the shower. But how can they truly know for sure if nobody hears it and can comment and/or feel good or bad about it? The same can be said for someone's coaching voice. If you don't try it out in front of people how can you know how effective or ineffective it can be?

When you get in front of your players you need to see what that voice can do. Again, I am not saying get out there and have a go (yell at) at your players, not at all. What I am saying is that perhaps you feel unsure of what you have to say as it pertains to your session. Perhaps you feel new and, as a result, do not want to lay it out there with being demanding from your session or holding people accountable. Nonsense, get out there and try it out. You will hopefully see some ideas and situations below where you can develop your voice in order to teach your players how to play. Get out there and do it. You cannot get better without trying stuff, so try it.

Use the Tone in Your Voice

Staying with my singing analogy from above: when singers sing and move you to feel something they do not stay monotone; they are loud and soft (and, of course, other things as well). Sometimes when the play gets stale a coach might raise his voice in order to see if he or she can raise the level of the players or raise the energy level. Other times a coach will be soft with his or her players when they need to be calm. Below are some suggestions for when and how to use your tone to ensure your presence is felt:

Maintain focus in training: Sometimes players get squirrelly. When players lose their focus in training sometimes they need that loud voice — aimed in the general direction of the group — to ensure they stay on track. I have seen many good coaches do this by initially yelling "stop" or "freeze," then use a soft voice to deliver a question of "do you think this is of quality?" Once that change in tone comes, and the point has been made, back to business.

Maintain calmness: Sometimes players are affected by the pressure of the game or situation. In those situations, when everything else is fast, out of control and unpredictable, a soft calm voice from you, the coach, indicates to all that it may be crazy out there but in here and with you all we are in control. This is a great way to ensure you are not only building that calm but also a way to build their understanding that they too can be calm in these pressure situations.

Maintain discipline: Players will break rules and must be held accountable. A coach with presence could come in screaming and yelling but not sure that really teaches anything nor does it lends itself to his presence. Coming in and softly asking that question of do you think that is acceptable? And if not, it shows that player that there are expectations and poor discipline will not be tolerated.

Rally the troops and gather energy: Yes, sometimes players need to understand that the level at which they are training or playing is not good enough. Sometimes players are just not working hard enough and are lacking energy. They will look to you to give them that energy on some occasions, so give it to them. Come in with that energy level and a "Hey, we can do this." Raising the tone of your voice doesn't mean you are screaming at players but could mean that you come in with a raised voice and this effort isn't good enough, and if we can't get this right, it won't go well.

To get a player who has had a bad game/outing back on track: Again, using your tone is key. Many times players know that they had a shocker. The last thing they need is someone, namely you, having a go at them. Yes, get in their ear but do it in such a way that your tone is demanding but encouraging.

There are multiple ways to use the tone of your voice. However you use it, use it wisely to win the war, not the battle. Do not let your emotion get the best of you and ensure that you are using it to move that player along and get the most out of that player or team.

Talking With Someone vs At Someone

I frequently talk about the value of talking with players vs at players. I describe *talking with* players as the idea that you are speaking with them in a conversation such that they understand there is a dialogue here and that we are seeking answers to a common problem. There is a relationship there. Sure there may be times when you are having a go at what an athlete is doing or not doing, but they know you care. There is something about the way you speak that says even though you are having a go, I know we are in this together and it's a "we" vs an "I" project. If an athlete senses you don't care, or are in it for just you, the likelihood is that he or she will stop fighting for you and the cause.

Talking to players indicates a diatribe and indicates to athletes that you are only interested in getting your point across and likely not interested in who they are or what they have to say. There is a sense that the coach is looking right through the person to get to the athlete, that the coach isn't interested in the person but rather what he or she can give the coach at that time. It's a very selfish use of a voice and the words that are chosen and the way they are conveyed aren't seeking a result but rather a win in the battle. This is a cold endeavor and adds nothing to the presence of the coach.

Talking with a player is easy when it is just you and the player, but let's face it, talking with a player when there are dozens of others is difficult. Yes, it is difficult as a group is made up of individuals, and each of those individuals will want and or need a relationship with you at some point. Just like a good actor making you feel like he is touching your soul and your soul alone, so too will a good coach need to make a big room seem small. So does the coach do that?

Ask questions: Asking questions as you speak to groups provides the recipient the opportunity to be a part of that conversation. When you ask questions vs tell people what to do all the time the person on the other end doesn't just have to sit there and ingest the words like a baby bird and his mom's worms. The player gets to hear what you are saying but then gets to also think about a response. As the player gets to think about a response, he or she is now connected to the solution intimately, as it may be partly his or hers.

When people's solutions are partly their doing this drives a person's motivation from within. Later in the book I will talk about motivation. A central tenant in someone feeling motivated from within is to feel part of the group. One very quick way to do that is to include them in those solutions by asking questions such as "What do you think we should be doing differently?" Or, "Do you think that is good enough, why, why not?" Those can be global questions (to the group vs one person) and really get at the heart of talk "with" vs "at" as the person can singularly internalize that question and possible response.

__Avoid constantly telling people what to do:__ Yes, this is pretty much the opposite of what I said above but it bears saying this as well. When someone comes in and continues to preach do this, do that, it's never fun. Think about it, do you like to be told what to do all the time? What impact does it have? Likely it ensures you get the job done in the short run but in the long run it becomes someone else's impetus and, as a result, when push comes to shove and the player has to choose what to do, he or she may disengage.

Do not get me wrong. Sometimes you have to tell people what to do, but it is about managing those times. When there are details to be learned on the athletic field there will, of course, be times where you need to tell people what to do, but if it is all the time it becomes preachy. If it's preachy, players might tune out.

__Make eye contact:__ When a coach is giving a group talk, he or she is necessarily talking to the group. But of course the goal is to talk with the group. One way to do that is to work the room with your eyes. Your eyes need to catch as many of "their" eyes as possible. And not just catch their eyes but engage them for that all uncomfortable 1-2 seconds. Scan the room as you speak, ensuring you are touching base with each person as you deliver your information. As you do, the players will begin to feel as if you are talking with them vs at them.

Find out about the person: In order to talk with someone, you need to know who you are working with. Take time to get to know the person that you are managing. As I say many times, you coach people you don't coach athletes. If they are older players, find out their children's names, spouse's name, their likes, dislikes, birthdays. If they are younger players, use their names frequently. Endeavor to get to know what they like to eat, what their favorite shows are, who their favorite players are, etc. Really take the time to get to know details about who they are as a person and use this information with them as you greet them for the day.

When a person understands that you care about who they are, your words are heard differently. The player receiving your words as a coach is now hearing them from a person that has asked about who they are. As a result, the words are met with a this is a "we" project as opposed to a "you" vs "me" project. That simple receiving of information, even when received in a group, establishes a tone right away as there is a relationship there.

Talking "with" vs "at" is an art and is certainly much more than just these bullet points. You will see as we get to management and feedback that we will come back to some of these points and expand on them. All of these things will help you. Yes, manage and provide feedback, but also establish your presence as a coach.

3. Body Language

I admit I haven't always been a fan, or a believer in, the merits of analyzing body language. This was until I watched a Ted.com clip from Harvard Professor Amy Cuddy. Dr. Cuddy studies and researches, among other things, body language. Dr. Cuddy begins by discussing the research-based merits on one's body language and its impact on other people. She discusses how, for instance, physicians' body language impacts whether or not they will be sued or how a one-second view of politicians' faces by voters determined whether or not they will be elected. These examples by themselves show the impact of body language on one's presence and how that presence impacts others' reactions and actions.

Dr. Cuddy continues to talk about the impact of our body language on ourselves. That is to say, she sought to find an answer to the question of what does one's body language do for the person that is doing the body language-ing. In other words, when I curl up in a ball what does it do to me and perhaps, as a result, to others?

Dr. Cuddy discussed the impact of one's nonverbal expressions, specifically the impact of how one opens up and/or closes down. She shows how people lift their arms in a "V" (so both hands over their heads) when they feel powerful and/or win a race (see Usain Bolt when he wins a track race!). She then goes on to talk about how, when people feel powerless, they collapse and wrap their arms around themselves or rub their hands on their necks. The fascinating component here is that there are actually hormone changes in the person doing the body language-ing. Meaning, the body's chemicals are actually impacted, and differently, based on how one opens up or closes down with their bodies.

Specifically, Dr. Cuddy studied testosterone (dominance/confidence) and cortisol (stress hormone) levels in people as they held either a power pose (V or hands to sides as they stood straight up) or a nonpower pose (arms folded, curled up, arm on neck, etc.) in front of an authority figure for two minutes. She found that when people raised their hands and/or stood in power positions they ACTUALLY raised their own testosterone levels and decreased their cortisol levels. These people realized their dominance/confidence levels and got calmer, while those in curled-up positions had higher cortisol levels and lower testosterone — higher stress and lower confidence. Amazing results!

This is amazing not only because it impacts the person doing it but because, as she previously showed, one's body language impacts others' perception about us. If this is the case then we can really use this in our argument for how to incorporate body language into how one builds and maintains presence.

The big takeaways here are: 1) body language impacts us as a person, and we can fake it until we make it, and 2) our body language impacts others' views about us, so the trick is to ensure we practice opening up for greater periods of time where people can see this in order to make an impact on how they view our presence.

Self-Awareness

Self-awareness is simply one's ability to look within and be mindful about what he or she is doing and how "what" one is doing impacts others. A good way to think about self-awareness is think about you and then think about an all-knowing entity that is watching and knowing your every move and thought, then observing those items and how they impact others. If you could get all of this very accurate and unbiased data from someone who doesn't have a horse in the race, think how helpful it would be. They could tell you what you actually did (argued too much, didn't listen, shrugged your shoulders, rolled your eyes, made an assumption without hearing someone), and once you know this information you can really see what you did and how you did it and how it impacted people, in this case, your players. This is self-awareness.

I once worked with an elite coach who told me nobody at the top of their profession, apart from a self-elected king or dictator, can be great at what they do without some measure of self-awareness. His argument was that one must continually check in with one's self in order to see if what they are doing is helping them and others to be effective. This makes complete sense as it relates to one's coaching "presence" as if one wants to make an impact on people they must assess how, what and when they are doing what it is they are doing. This takes time and of course some specific doings to get.

**Use others:** Sometimes learning about oneself is gained by speaking with someone else. Is it truly self-awareness if someone else has to tell you about it? Well, yes and no. People have to learn to give themselves feedback. Sometimes augmented feedback (other given) is the way we learn to give ourselves that accurate information we use in time to be good.

Ask a trusted confidant to be that observer described above. Ask them to watch you in certain situations — what you are doing and how that is being interpreted by players and others. Ask them to do this on multiple occasions and over time you will see that it will make an impact on what you learn to be aware of in order to gain self-awareness and ultimately have presence.

Watch video: Watching yourself is not always fun, but it is revealing. When you watch yourself, and also watch others watch you, you will notice certain things happen. People will react to things that you do, or don't do. I would strongly suggest doing this in critical situations, as that is when we really give off those strong body language signs — for the good and for the bad.

Write in a journal: Writing down your thoughts in a timely fashion ensures more accurate recall or, well, reality. When you force yourself to write down what you did when, for instance, a player made a massive mistake, will help you get a sense of what actually may have led to either his or her continued slide through the game or his bounce-backness after the mistake and your reaction. Just as important as what happened is how you felt. Adding your emotion allows you to get a sense of the state you were in when you reacted the way you did. Again, all of these practices will help you gain better self-awareness in order to positively impact your presence as a coach.

Manage body language while you are talking: Many people use gestures when they talk. This animation is awesome when it's lending itself to your quality presence. But when it's not, it is detrimental and ineffective.

Sometimes self-awareness is simply about stopping yourself as you are talking and readjusting your thoughts and, as a result, also your body language. It can be as simple as saying to yourself, "Okay, what am I saying and what am I doing, and how is it impacting others?" Frequently this pause provides us that little moment to change direction if we need it. This pause in words is critical because our words often dictate our bodily actions as we talk.

Thinking while you are talking/gesturing takes time. A good way to learn to do this is by completing your statement or direction and letting your players get on with what you want them to get on with. Once they are off doing what they need to be doing, you have a moment to collect your thoughts. Then, simply do a quick recall of what you just did. Was it what you wanted? If not, then what could you have done differently? Once you learn to do this after you talk, try it when you are talking: can you notice what you are doing when you are doing it? Can you change it midstream? Try it, you'll be surprised how good you get at it in time.

Be Aware of Your Limbs

Dr. Cuddy discusses how certain arm/hand placements display weakness, discomfort and a general nonopenness about the person. She talks about folded arms, hands wrapping around one's own neck, or one arm folded across the body while the other wraps the neck, all of which are signs of weakness and discomfort in one's situation. In essence all of these gestures are closing the person off to the people he or she is talking with. This type of body language says "I have no presence and there is no need to listen to me as I am not too comfortable with what I am saying or doing right now." No presence!

On the other hand, think about that person with presence and who uses his or hands and arms to say "Listen to me as what I have to say means something." People with presence will open their bodies up when they are speaking. Dr. Cuddy discusses how this is actually a power pose and says to people "I know what I am talking about." In essence it is an outward display of comfort and confidence! Examples include hands up to the side when talking in front of people to invite them in when they ask a question, pounding one hand with the other as one talks, placing one's thumb and pointer finger together and shaking them back and forth (see Bill Clinton in the famous "I did not..." speech), pointing to different places on the field where perhaps a player should go or could go. In each of those cases they are opening their body up as they are talking — adding to their presence and to your belief in them.

These are just some small examples of body language — and in essence nonverbal communication (which I tackle in more depth later) — and the impact it will have on your presence. Again, small examples as there are many, many more. The takeaway message in this area is be aware of whether or not you are closing yourself off or inviting people in with your body language. Keep in mind that when you close people off or display weakness this is not lending to one's presence.

Use Your Eyes Wisely

Eyes are the window to one's soul, and in this case also the window into one's presence. When I was a kid I had the good fortune to play for a sensational German coach named Wolfgang Weber. He had presence in many ways. One of the things that gave him presence was his eyes — and how and when he used them.

Wolf had built up plenty of presence over time but his eyes are what told you that you had really crossed the line or had done something well. If you made a mistake that shouldn't have been made he would give you this look that spoke volumes. Sometimes it said "That shouldn't be happening." Sometimes it said "Really?" Sometimes it said, "If you don't get it right we are going to have some real issues." On the flip side when you did something well and his eyes raised it seemed to also raise you and your level. Whatever my interpretation was, the truth was that his eyes said things to me and others that he didn't need to say aloud, they established what needed to get done and help established his presence.

To be sure, in most cases eyes are only effective once the person's presence has been established through actions or words. That is to say, as I listened to Wolf he built up his presence through verbal feedback as he coached us both on and off the field. But as he did this he would also use his eyes as he spoke, looking at us in different ways, as he delivered his information. These well-placed glances provided us an opportunity to hear him without hearing him.

So eyes can be used for any coach who is establishing his presence and wishing to deliver information and build up his presence without saying a thing. Again, we will talk more about this later in the feedback section (and also a bit in the management section) when we talk about nonverbal communication. But for now, here are a few examples of how to establish and maintain presence using your eyes:

Look at people after you deliver information: Having presence means really letting people know you are talking with them vs at them. The way people receive information is, yes, through words, but also through those windows into one's soul. So in this case as you are talking with your athletes take that second after you talk to look them right in their eyes and check not only for understanding but also for a notice that they understand you care that they hear your message. This allows the learner to connect with you as that three to four second pause where eyes connect ensures that they know that you are bought in to them vs into just their contribution to the sport.

Scan the room and wait: I will revisit this in a management discussion again but it's worth noting here as well that as you talk with a group, if you fail to look at entire sections of the room and engage their eyes you may be missing out on an opportunity to build your presence. Scanning the room as you talk ensures that your eyes are meeting up with others' eyes. As you deliver messages to entire groups, catching their eyes ensures that they understand that you are checking for understanding, as it is critical that everyone hears you. This sends the message that all are accountable and that you will ensure that each one of them hears and gets stuff done. This lends to your presence in a way that just words would not.

Take a second to look away when you are delivering something of thought: Perhaps this one sounds odd but players want to know that you have thought about what you want to say before you say it. Moreover, they want to know that you are rational and reasonable. As you are communicating with people your message and something that is thought-provoking comes up, pause. Stop and think about it. As you do this, your eyes can look outward or upward. Yes, sounds silly, but people watch what you do and as you do this you take that second to really ponder what you are about to say; more importantly they see you do this. This lends to presence as it shows them you are thoughtful and patient in your choices to these types of questions.

Eyes are very powerful tools. Using your eyes as a coach to look at people in their eyes is the surest way to let someone know you mean business, care about them, or convey many a thought that is personal. But, be thoughtful how you use those eyes because they really can allow people an opportunity to get to understand more about you without you saying anything at all. The biggest takeaway point here is that your eyes as a coach can be used to help build your presence in many ways. Use them wisely.

4. Be a Person First, Not a Coach First

Some of the best stories about great coaches — their presence and as a result their greatness — do not occur on the field or court but off of it. One of the most successful examples of this type of coach is the National Football League's Tony Dungy. Coach Dungy had a very successful career as a coach to the tune of 28 years in the NFL, two AFC championships and, of course, a Super Bowl Championship with the Indianapolis Colts. But more importantly about Coach Dungy was that he was a teacher of men and this simple approach allowed the extremely soft-spoken man to have a huge presence in a league dominated by overly loud, aggressive personalities, especially at the head coach position.

Mr. Dungy was purported to have had a simple philosophy: that coaches are teachers and that a coach's responsibility extends far beyond the football field. He espoused things like a person's family is extremely important, that treating the best player and the 33rd best player as if they were each as massively important to the cause as the other, and that screaming and yelling at someone wasn't necessarily the best way to get them to respond. Each of these ideas promoted the notion that he was a person and cared about each and every other person.

This appears to be the crux of his presence and who he was as a person. Players and assistant coaches have praised his style of leadership and coaching. Coach Dungy appears to have been able to get players to listen and follow by, yes, having a great plan (content), but also by establishing a relationship with that person so that his presence, and in the end, his message came across. Coach Dungy had a very close working relationship with his staff and also made a great impact across the NFL — spawning a multitude of future head coaches — again, yes, because he had a great plan but mostly it would appear because of his presence and the way he approached people.

Being a person first is essentially reminding you to be sure to treat people as people and not as athletes or commodities. It is a reminder that, of course you want them to get to a certain level, but at what expense? People (athletes included) will respond better when they know you love them and care about who they truly are. If they understand this, you can really push (with) them to get to that next level.

I contend that athlete, when they are young, will remember very little about the minutia of your session or game instruction. What they will remember is who you were and how you were with them during practices, games and times off of the field. In good times and bad, did you have a positive impact on them as a person?

In the end, being a person first adds to one's presence because we are all people and when one person (especially in a competitive environment) cares enough about another person, they will do the same. Take time to get to know all of your athletes as people. (I will talk about this in great detail later in the management section.) It is critical. Getting a sense of the person as an individual is a first step into establishing a relationship with him or her. And having a relationship with each athlete is a first step toward a common goal. When the athlete knows you have a goal in mind for you and him or her, he or she will "buy-in" and this "buy-in" means you have made your presence felt.

Let's end where we began — get a picture of Sir Alex Ferguson. Can you see him and his larger-than-life presence? To be fair you could probably do this with your high school or college coach that you felt had presence, or even you. Can you see them handling the session or game like a good actor would, making you believe? Can you see and hear them and their voice or body language making an impact on you and the group? And, of course, don't you remember the person that they were toward you and your teammates?

Building presence takes time and a lot of experience(s), as we will discuss later. As a new, emerging coach, try these and other things that help you establish who you are as a person and a coach. These will help you along your path. But of course, to be good at this stuff you need to do it; so do it!

Chapter 4

Environment

A great environment is different depending on who you ask or what you are. A great environment for plants and trees is one with enough sun, water and perhaps a little love to help them grow. A great environment for artists might be a place with lots of inspiration, some paint or clay, and plenty of time to create something awe-inspiring. A great environment for babies to thrive has plenty of food, opportunities to explore the environment and, of course, plenty of encouragement and love as they grow.

We could go on and on with examples of great environments for living things. If we were to explore examples of great environments where living things developed, we would see a lot of the same things. We would see a place with expectations to grow and develop, a steady dose of nourishment in the form of food or information, a place that provided inspiration and challenges in order to stimulate growth and development toward an ultimate goal. Think about it — if you did this anywhere with any living thing, you would have something that, in the end, reached its potential, whatever that was.

But, of course, the devil is in the details. Let's look at a couple of examples where this great environment plays out. We will explore one in business and one in sport.

Larry and Sergey's
Excellent Adventure

How many of you have heard of Larry Page or Sergey Brin? My guess is that many of you haven't. In 1997 they two were Ph.D. students at Stanford University studying computer science. But we perhaps know them better for what they did in 1998 when they started a little company called Google. Yes, we know more about Google than perhaps about its founders but my initial point here, is that an environment of expectations, excellence and creativity is started by someone, or something, and when refined over time can turn into something very special and very successful.

Google is a worldwide phenomenon that has created and maintained unparalleled online products and services. Many of the things Google is doing — from search engines to Gmail, from Google Maps to Google glasses, are changing how we live our lives. Germane to this conversation, though, is the unique environment that Google has set up to ensure not only productivity but creativity in an ever-changing field.

So what does Google have to do with coaching sports? Not unlike sport, Google finds itself and its employees having to perform every day, under pressure, and in an endeavor that is constantly changing. Moreover, it is a demanding job that requires that managers or systems implemented by managers ensure its employees maintain motivation, all while being competitive to find that "what's next" and deliver quality products in a timely manner. Sounds to me exactly like sport apart from something physical. So the question is, what type of environment are they creating that is ensuring this type of quality?

Google appears to have created an environment that sets high standards for creating very thought-filled, innovative products and empowers its employees to do it. The first thing to notice about Google is that it has a director of People Operations. In essence, this is its human resource department but so much more. Its motto is "find them, grow them and keep them." Straight from Google's website it says "Whether recruiting the next great Googler, refining our core programs, developing talent or simply looking for ways to inject more fun into the lives of our Googlers, we bring a data-driven approach that is reinventing the human resources field."

Google treats its employees as people — offering them opportunities to develop themselves and who they are as well as offering them certain development opportunities like gym memberships, a voice in the direction of certain projects, and access to information about the direction of the company. In addition, Google offers its employees the opportunity to spend 20 percent of their workday on things they want to do. Can you imagine providing an environment where you are demanding that people be creative, but giving them the opportunity to do it with stuff they want to do? This could lead to real innovation.

What this boils down to is that Google ensures its employees are treated as people so that they have the opportunity to create great products. This idea of "taking care of the person" is key and gets at the heart of providing an environment that is establishing motivation to be productive because you want to vs because you have to. But let's not confuse this with a country club — there are real expectations at Google, not just projects for fun-sies.

Google is an industry leader and not by accident. Employees are expected to deliver products just like every other company. One of the founder's mottos is that "great isn't good enough." This says all you need to know about the goal of Google and its products - the products and, as a result, the people need to be better than great, they need to be exceptional. Google is after something beyond greatness, and it would seem it isn't really going to be content with anything less than that, and that's okay. But, the interesting thing here is that all of this drive to be great is being driven by a company that is helping you the employee be great at the same time.

It would seem then that if we could find an environment in sport that was looking to develop the person first, as well as ensure the utmost quality in performances, that would be a good thing. Wouldn't it make sense? Let's look at one of the greatest sport examples of this philosophy — let's look at John Wooden.

John Wooden's
Environment of Excellence

John Wooden created an environment of excellence for his players and his programs. Wooden is widely considered one of the greatest coaches of all time. Coach Wooden was the basketball coach at UCLA from 1948 to 1975, and he won ten national championships and 88 consecutive games, and impacted the lives of countless young men with his teaching and leadership.

Coach Wooden was said to be an incredible coach. He had detailed exercises and drills to coach his brand of basketball. He also had incredibly unique ways of teaching people how to play basketball. In fact, some of his teaching methods, namely the pyramid of success, are actually used in business schools to teach people to be successful business people. This environment that he created based on this pyramid of success was one built on expectations of fundamentals, building good people, being motivated and confident and on being a thought-filled person.

John Wooden's environment of expectations was built on his pyramid of success. The pyramid started with this redefinition of success: "Success is a peace of mind which is a direct result of self-satisfaction in knowing you made the effort to become the best you are capable of becoming." To this end, Coach Wooden designed his pyramid around this definition. ·

At the base of the pyramid you will see that he has values and virtues of a good person. This foundation is at the heart of Coach Wooden's environment in that building good people is what it is all about.

Next he gets into ambition and motivation in order to get after it. This level ensures that there is intent and initiative to move slowly toward the success at the top of
the pyramid.

He then moves into adaptability and honesty within each person. This level has values such as condition (mental and physical) as well as skill and team. This level is about the expectations and hard work one must put in to be great. It is also about thinking and one's ability to change in order to be great.

He slowly moves up the pyramid into continued thinking and an ability to perform under pressure. He uses words like "resourcefulness" and "confidence" to ensure people understand that, yes, hard work, and yes, being a good person, are important, but one needs to have poise and build confidence if one is to be successful.

Finally, he reaches the top where he talks about competitiveness in order to reach the pinnacle, which is success. But he talks about this competitiveness relative to one's self vs others. This is critical as it sets the tone for personal expectations and working at those every single time you are out there.

If you look at this pyramid it truly is a blueprint for an environment of excellence and what it takes to be great. Coach Wooden's environment was built on a foundation of expectations for success. He moved toward those expectations with meticulousness and care-filled-ness through daily discussions, lessons, routines, exercises and planned ways of moving his players along from average to great. But of course his environment started with a basic premise — be a good person.

Bill Walton, one of Coach Wooden's former players who turned into a lifetime friend had this to say about him: "Coach Wooden never talked about winning and losing, but rather about the effort to win. He rarely talked about basketball, but generally about life. He never talked about strategy, statistics or plays, but rather about people and character. Coach Wooden never tired of telling us that once you become a good person, then you have a chance of becoming a good basketball player."[7]

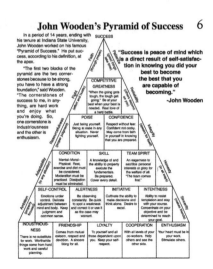

Coach Wooden appeared to have expectations that his players were good people first. This is genius, as it says to these people: "Hey, I care about you and how I can help you, but also how you can help us be great." (Sounds a bit like Google, no?) The thing is that by starting here he establishes this base and then works methodically to drive at other things in his environment like details and thinking within sessions, ensuring players are motivated and confident and, finally, that what you are doing is all leading up to ensuring a great product — both on and off the court.

Wooden was famous for establishing an environment that asked for nothing short of his players' best effort, EVERY day. If I tried to pull a best quote, story, book or article written about his attention to detail, quality methods, and focus on being great I would probably still be digging. Take a second and Google John Wooden and you will find countless descriptions and firsthand accounts from his players about the environment of expectations he set up in his practices and drills to ensure the players were maximally prepared. You would also find that all along the way Coach Wooden treated his players with dignity, improved motivation and confidence, taught them life lessons and ensured they were becoming better people as well as part of the larger goal — which in many cases was a championship basketball team. The pyramid is truly a philosophy that, when adhered to, creates an environment of excellence.

If you look at these two examples they are not that different. Each of the examples of great environments had expectations of excellence and a place with massive amounts of communication, as well as opportunities to develop as people as well as athletes/new-product-builders, and plenty of opportunities for thinking and problem solving — all in the name of making a great product. These are great environments. But how can we take all of these items and ensure we as coaches can create our own environment of excellence?

I've broken these things down into three categories, and items within those categories, that great coaches do to create a great environment. If you do these things as well, you will be well on your way to creating a great environment in which your athletes thrive.

I. Creating a Positive and Demanding Environment

1. Setting and Ensuring Expectations

The cornerstone of any great education, sport or business plan is that there are standards and expectations for which to reach. These standards and expectations are critical in guiding everyone's focus and daily work habits. In essence, these are the goals and objectives toward which people are striving. Every classroom, team or business can have these goals, but very few of them drive toward reaching these goals.

The great coach (Wooden) or great business (Google) ensures that its players or employees are working to reach these expectations. They set goals, quotas, point total expectations, attempts, etc., so that their people are constantly reaching. They ensure that their employees are not confusing activity with accomplishment, as the latter is the only thing that leads to success.

Focused Training vs Participation

Great coaches ensure that the environment that they create has people that are training to improve as opposed to just simply showing up and going through the motions. Much has been written about the 10,000 hour rule and that that is what is needed in order to be great. It is true that doing something for 10,000 hours will likely make you better as you are doing more of it — whatever "it" is. But better doesn't mean great, because if you are doing something wrong for that 10,000 hours, then you are just worse at it. In addition, if for instance, in many hours of that 10,000 hours you are simply showing up and putting, say, 50 percent effort in, then really what you have at the end of 10,000 hours is actually 10,000 hours of average work that you have done over and over. This is akin to having a book and reading paragraph after paragraph but not remembering a thing — yes you have read a chapter but you really haven't gained any knowledge, you just got further into the book.

There are a few exceptional books that discuss this concept in greater detail. One is called *The Talent Code*. This book (among other things) explores the idea of "deep practice" and it is actually this deep practice that leads to the greatest improvements. The author chronicles great musicians and athletes, and talks about how the most improvement in the least amount of time takes place when they get into this zone of "deep practice." He explores in great detail how these deep practice sessions actually change the neurological pathways that allow, in essence, messages to fire the muscles that lead to more refined skills and, in the end, greater performance levels.

It's one thing to know this information about deep practice or focused practice vs participation and another thing entirely to ensure our athletes do it. So how can we get our athletes to do this? Below are some suggestions I have seen good coaches do to ensure focused training vs participation in order to help create this great environment.

Hold them accountable: Focused training doesn't occur on accident, so ensure your athletes are held accountable. Accountability is critical if someone wants to improve on, say, passing or zonal defending or scoring. If players are not held accountable to the details within each of those exercises, then how can they be expected to perform them well in games?

Holding people accountable doesn't mean screaming at them and demanding perfection at all times. There are some times where players must make mistakes in order to improve — it is key. But even in those times you can demand that they are working their hardest and engaging in what at that time would be a very cognitive approach to their task (meaning thinking about every step in the skill or tactic). You can ask of them high focus even if there are a lot of errors — this ensures attention to detail and it ensures focused training vs simple participation.

All on task: This is also an accountability issue but one that I think coaches allow way too often. Sometimes we do not look around the room or field enough to see that are all engaged. A coach should always ensure that when he is going over an activity or drill or game plan that his players are listening. If he doesn't, then someone is missing something.

Take that second to look up and scan that room to ensure all eyes are on you. By using those eyes (presence) to take three to five quiet seconds to see if all are listening, you have just indicated that this is critical and ALL should listen. Again, focused participation by all, not some.

**Do more of less:** Sometimes we have so much to say that we try to get it all out in one session. This makes it hard to focus fully and ensure maximum information is received because of the sheer volume you may have included in that practice. Many times if we simply take a moment to see where our athletes are in the learning process and give them what they can handle, we can really get at that information and hammer it home as opposed to losing them in the session and they get lost as a result.

By doing less we are actually ensuring a focused practice. Think about it, how much information can you handle at once? Everybody is different but experts say most of us can only remember four things at once in a short amount of time. Now obviously, don't take that literally but do keep in mind that focusing on a few things vs numerous things is a good place to start when ensuring focused practice vs participation.

**Tell/show them what you are going to do before you do it:** Many athletes at various levels (pro, college, youth) function much better when they know what is coming. I have seen many great coaches tell their athletes (using words, a white board, an iPad or computer and screen) what the session is going to be that day and what the expectations are in the session. This is really including athletes in what is going on and where they need to be at the end. By doing this you are maximizing buy-in and as a result likely focused training as well.

2. Ensure Athletes Are Reaching

Part of ensuring a positive and demanding environment is

providing a safe, yet challenging place, where athletes are reaching to improve every day. Reaching for something better is critical to an athlete's everyday existence; the best players in the world are never satisfied with their current form. As you look and listen to athletes in various sports at the top of their game (Cristiano Ronaldo, Kevin Durant, Serena Williams) you will see and hear some of the same things. They understand that, yes they are playing well, but that there are still areas in which they are improving. It is this pursuit of excellence and constant improvement that drives these athletes. But not every athlete is born this way.

Some athletes (from the pro to the very young) will not reach for that extra something, for various reasons. Some won't reach because they lack confidence, while others won't reach for fear of failure, and still others won't reach because they lack that desire to persist in the face of difficulty. As coaches we should strive to create this environment that rewards persistence and effort and sees failures as opportunities as opposed to end points. The truth is that the more an athlete learns that he or she must fail and then get back up to actually get great at what he or she does, the better it is in the long run.

Creating an environment that encourages reaching is critical and actually drives that athlete (to do on their own vs us telling them) more toward our first item under ensuring expectations — that of focused training vs participation. I will talk about this more below soon when we set up an environment that rewards the athlete for his or her daily pursuit of improvement, as opposed to being perfect all the time, we are actually decreasing the amount of pressure and lack of control we are placing on the athlete.

Think about it, when you know the expectation is improving, say your backswing vs winning every point, you feel like you have more control. Compare this feeling to finding out your playing partner for the day is Roger Federer (seventeen-time Grand Slam-winning tennis legend). You are done before you even start! This environment that you set up that rewards for reaching gives more control to the athlete. This control provides an opportunity for that athlete to drive harder at what he or she is doing because it is a choice. This drive, as a result, will help the athlete move toward focused training vs simple participation.

So — how to create an environment that helps athletes reach? The items below will absolutely help you create an environment that encourages reaching. You will see that I talk about redefining success, persistence, a focus on improving vs constant perfection, as well as stress and why it's a good thing (to which I briefly allude to above). Each of these things is deeply rooted in research on high performance in sports, and if you put these in your coaching repertoire, I assure you they will lead to a greater environment for athletes and, as a result, improved performance.

Redefine Success in Your Practices

Your environment must have expectations for success. But how will you define success? Is success always an end product — a win, a place (1st, 2nd, etc.), or improvement relative to someone else? There is nothing wrong with having expectations to win or beat someone else, but if that's all you reward then am I a failure every time I don't win? If so, how will athletes grow in training if they lose?

When you have an environment that always defines success as being the best or a win vs someone else it may actually hinder improvement. Yes, they will have a target for which to strive — I want to beat that person or be the best at that move — but what happens if they don't get it? Do they persist? Some will, some won't (I will talk about this later). For those who do not persist, they will quit. In addition, perhaps only some can reach this concrete standard — as if you are doing one-on-ones to get to a winner and a loser, 50 percent of people automatically fail with no hope of success in this limited definition. Can success be defined as something different than just an end point and still be demanding?

Try defining success differently than just a concrete end point. Try defining success as the attempt for greatness. Define success so athletes can be rewarded and feel successful if they are working toward improvement and are focused on self-referenced success vs beating someone else all the time. This, in the end, will set up very high expectations but realistic and reachable ones as well.

The truth is that if you set up an environment in your trainings that views success as improving and learning compared with just winning or beating others, then athletes can feel comfortable reaching ALL the time. Think about it — you are asking me to improve a skill (perhaps that backhand that we referred to earlier) but I am playing a VERY good player. And if I don't win (because that's how you have defined success), you are going to praise the other guy and just simply have a go at me and tell me that's not good enough. More importantly than your praise is that I am not going to try that backhand as that's not my "go-to" swing when I NEED to win. My "go-to" swing is a forehand, and as a result, that's what I am more inclined to do when the pressure is on to win.

People will not try things and reach when they know they are being judged on a result. In fact, when the pressure is on to perform, they will most often go to their dominant response. This will, of course be, that "go-to" thing (forehand, a move to their right as opposed to going left), which also may not be the right choice (or technique to use at that time). This choice is basically made for them as they are not encouraged to reach but rather to win by any means necessary, which doesn't build a diverse bag of tricks when the pressure is truly on.

Redefining success in terms of attempts vs results is critical to reaching. Take time in your sessions to ensure your environment includes multiple opportunities for success. This success should be based on attempting what it is you are asking them to improve on in that exercise. In addition, it should be on their improvement vs beating someone else. This will ensure that the less quality player has plenty of opportunities to reach and get better. Moreover, it will also help the elite person as perhaps she is winning far too easily and isn't really trying new stuff either.

Develop Persistence – Get Them To Compete!

Persistence literally means to continue steadfastly or firmly in some state, purpose, course of action, especially in spite of opposition. These qualities, for someone striving to reach and improve, are key. We have just discussed redefining success in terms of improving and learning vs winning or just beating someone else in order to help ensure our great environment. The next step in this is helping someone understand how to take full advantage of your redefinition by helping the person develop persistence.

Okay, so you have redefined success in your sessions, ensuring you are rewarding improvement and learning vs just beating somebody else, but are they taking full advantage of this opportunity to reach? Meaning you have set the stage for their safe passageway to reach further out on the tree limb to grab that fruit on the end of it by telling them it's okay. But how can you get them to actually get out on that limb after perhaps they have fallen once before? What can you do? What are we asking them to do?

People with persistence are actually doing something we do every day, and some of us more than others. We "continue" very "firmly" with a real "purpose" especially vs an "opposition." We compete! Really, when an athlete is being *persistent*, what we are essentially saying is that he or she is *competing* to be *successful.*

Setting up an environment where there is competition is absolutely critical. Competition at any age is a major key to improvement. When we as coaches set up an environment where athletes are challenged to reach out on that limb — to compete, to persist — in order to improve and get better (our redefined success), we are setting the stage for their pursuit of something better. The key here is that we are not saying compete in order to beat that other person (many athletes do that on their own and that's okay). What we are saying is compete, against yourself and your personal best, to go ahead and reach on out there for that tasty fruit on the edge of the limb.

When you provide an environment where you challenge someone to improve, and you are there to encourage and teach them during this pursuit, you are basically building persistence by encouraging competitiveness within themselves. For athletes to be challenged with certain goals or a number of attempts at a skill, or improving on a certain time (relative to them) or improvement on a certain skill such that they can do it more proficiently in games or practices, they are competing. When they are rewarded often by actual results (better skill/time/ choices, etc.) or words of encouragement, you are building their base of persistence. This environment of persistence is critical for any athlete given the amount of times they will actually fail in their sport.

Let's get real here, sports are based on winning and losing at the higher levels like older club teams/high school, college and professional. Yes, true, but critical to this pursuit of wins is one's ability to bounce back after losses and focus on what one did well or poorly. If a coach comes in screaming about "we need to win this," or "if you don't win you are out," there are a number of athletes who will have absolute shockers and may experience very high anxiety (more on this later), will fail and quit. There are many reasons why they quit, but a major one is that they aren't having successes. And let's face it, everyone wants success. But interestingly enough the majority, if not all, of the coaches that win a great deal, do not talk about winning. They talk about improving and learning, persisting and competing — every day. The reason for this is because wins don't come as a result of focusing on the win, they come as a result of a relentless pursuit of improving on the things that it takes to win — this takes reaching!

Let's continue to deal in reality as some would argue that competition at a young age is not good — I would say that is absolute nonsense. Kids compete constantly — monkey bars, studying for spelling tests, playing tag and, yes, even in sports at seven and eight years old. And encouraging kids to improve on these pursuits is great. Of course, my advice is to look at competition differently with children, as they are not the same as adults, clearly!

Creating an environment with children where you gently encourage improvement is encouraging them to compete. You are setting expectations by asking them to improve when they make a mistake. Ask them to try it again, encourage improvement on the process steps it takes to say do the move or shoot the ball or try that stroke. Once they try it, reward it with a "that's great keep trying that." See what happens. They will, over time, learn a healthy approach to competition and develop persistence, guaranteed. You must work to find the level that the player is at so you know how high to set the improvement bar so he or she can see improvement.

Here are a few reminders when it comes to helping you create an environment of expectations where athletes are developing persistence in their sport:

Get athletes to compete against themselves: Encourage athletes to compete against themselves by having them recall their previous attempt and what they could have done better. Some will buck this trend very quickly, instead choosing to focus on the result, or how they suck or some other extreme. It's who they are (Google achievement goal theory — namely, ego-oriented athlete), but your influence and focus on providing multiple chances to improve personally can change this disposition; it'll take time, but it works.

Reward concrete things in games where they compete against themselves: Competing against players in practices is often unavoidable and frequently very good. Multiple sports have games that are 1v1 or 2v2 and so on where there is a result. No problem, all is okay. But add a different element in there. Whatever you are working on, provide opportunities for points via that skill. For example, you may be working on passing the ball and getting it back (combination play). If teams do that, 1) verbally reward that often, and 2) reward it with additional points in the game in which they are playing.

Call out the behavior if it's not good enough: Remember we are still talking about ensuring expectations here and being competitive to ensure quality is critical. When athletes aren't putting in the requisite effort they should be challenged to do so. A "do you think that was your best effort" statement can go a long way to setting expectations of persistence and ensuring the environment.

When athletes fail vs someone, remind them of the goal: Some athletes are VERY tough on themselves. This isn't bad — it just needs to be managed. The athletes who, when they compete can't help but make it a me vs you thing, will very often thrive off of this mentality in competition, when they win. But, when they lose, they may not have the appropriate coping skills to manage this. So, when they compete, and they lose, they are upset, no worries. It's a constant reminder of the goal to reach to be better, to persist after failure to ensure improvement. This takes many repetitions — many!

Helping the Athlete See Stress As An Opportunity vs A Potential Catastrophe

Some stress when reaching is good but of course too much stress is not good. As an example, when I am explaining this to any adults who have been in college, all I have to do is ask if anyone out there remembers when they started their end-of-year term paper, when it was assigned or closer to when it was due? Most people's response is that they waited until a few days before and when they started to feel the pressure a bit. Once this initial stress kicked in they got after it, a healthy amount of stress kicked in, got them going and even provided that spark to be creative and reach to create a quality paper. But if they waited too long, that stress was anything but healthy and usually turned into anxiety. And, once that anxiety came into play, they ceased to reach as they wrote the paper and settled for anything that would get the job done.

If athletes are to reach, there must be a healthy amount of discomfort as they begin to reach. If there isn't this healthy stress, then they aren't learning anything that is out of their comfort zone. Rather, they are playing it safe as they are scared to get out of their bubble. In fact, a system cannot grow if it is not stressed out. That is to say, when an athlete is physiologically wanting to get bigger lifting weights, if he is to actually get stronger, he must put heavier weights, more reps, different exercises, etc., in a methodical and safe way in order to gain more strength. He must stress the system out. In order for athletes to develop as people and as athletes their systems must also be stressed out. But your environment must ensure that the focus is on ensuring this safe stress vs unsafe stress.

An oft-repeated phrase that I use when I am working with athletes or students is that you need to "learn to get comfortable being uncomfortable." This is basically telling those people that, look, I am going to ask you to do a lot of things that you may not be all that okay with — okay — it's still going to happen. And because it is going to happen I am warning you now, learn to look at these times as opportunities to improve as opposed to potential catastrophes. Now, the trick is to ensure you provide consequences that show the athlete that these indeed are opportunities vs catastrophes. We will get into that later, but first a few terms related to stress so we are on the same page.

Good stress is called eustress and is associated with a term called arousal. Bad stress is called distress and is often associated with anxiety. Some of the way athletes perceive stress is innate — but a lot of it has to do with the environment you create, what you reward, and how you define success. And, what happens is that when an athlete stresses out too much his or her good stress (arousal) turns to bad stress (anxiety) and he or she falls off the cliff and everything goes south. They freak out a bit, their heart rates increase and they engage in things like negative self-talk — and in the end they persist less, compete less, and, yes, *reach* less (for a really good picture of this, Google "Yerkes Dodson inverted U"). So it is critical that you create an environment that increases the likelihood that athletes look at critical situations as opportunities (good stress) vs potential catastrophes (anxiety).

So, how do we create good stress so that athletes want to reach vs do not want to reach? Well, really we have already hit some major ways to do this in the subsections above entitled "*Redefine success*" and "*Develop Persistence – get them to compete!*" Those are starters, but sometimes it's about helping athletes make sense of failures or stressful situations (FYI, this is also "Management" stuff that we will address later as we are managing the person and his/her ability to stay on track). Here are a few ideas to ensure a great environment by helping players manage stress in order to reach.

Help players be self-aware: There are a few times that I will bring up self-awareness, as it is critical to being great. But in this case it is critical that players understand that stress is even occurring. Sometimes athletes are not in tune with their thoughts and the fact that those thoughts and feelings are actually hindering their pursuit of something more. Getting athletes to learn to be aware and to acknowledge feelings like being upset, frustrated, and even lost or disparaged is a starting point. Sometimes acknowledging these things can set an athlete on a path to change.

Help players identify and change self-talk: What players say to themselves can negatively impact their focus on reaching and trying things by increasing stress. Perhaps they will say to themselves "why should I do that" or "I always lose" or "I always fail" or "I suck at that so why should I even try?" These things are preventing reaching as they are creating undue stress on the athlete — sometimes prior to even engaging in the activity.

Help the athlete identify (this is like building awareness) what he or she is saying to himself or herself. Once they do this they can hopefully make the link that this is holding them back from reaching. Then work to reprogram this talk by first getting them to make the connection that success in your environment is redefined — it is their focus on constant improvement that's what is expected here. This will provide a measure of control and perhaps lead to less stress, leading to more reaching, which is what you are asking for in the end anyway.

Encourage them to approach correctness vs avoid wrongness (less "stop doing that" more "start/keep doing that"): When people try to stop smoking they sometimes succeed. But when people try to stop smoking and try to start doing something else (like exercising or chewing gum) they succeed more often. When one is approaching doing something new vs avoiding doing something wrong one is going after something new — one has to persist and reach for that something as opposed to try to not do something. This is a very powerful difference in the mind as there is that measure of control here which decreases stress and increases the focus on "I can do this vs I can't stop that."

So your role is to reward athletes for trying to do things right vs punish them for doing things wrong. The more times you can catch them doing good the more they can approach correctness vs avoid wrongness. Then, when they do fall (which they will) the stress is less and their desire to persist is there, as is their desire to reach.

3. Ensure Details

Bill Belichick is one of the winningest NFL coaches of all time. He has won over 200 games, including five AFC Championships and three Super Bowls. By all accounts he creates an environment of excellence for his athletes in multiple ways to ensure these results. What Coach Belichick is most renowned for, though, is his meticulous attention to detail — for trainings as well as games.

Follow almost any player (or opposing coach and their thoughts) that played for the coach and you will read story after story about his relentless pursuit of details when preparing his players to play. Players frequently describe Coach Belichick as demanding of your intelligence, concentration, effort and physical engagement. He purportedly runs exercises, tells you why and when they are to be run, and then does them over and over until the details are engrained in the players. Moreover, it is said that no matter how well they are run (and this is key), he understands that there is always room for improvement.

You cannot create an environment of excellence without ensuring attention to details. Quick time out: In this same section you'll recall I said redefine success with a focus on improvement and learning vs outcome, and reward effort, but now I am saying get the details right? You should be asking the question, can you do both? Of course my answer will be yes, but the key is in the phrasing — both of the goal and with your athletes.

The goal should be the pursuit of details, and that goal shouldn't be compromised. But of course how one sets up that environment to ensure their athletes are striving for those details is key. Will you say to them get it right or you fail and that's it? Or will you say this is the expectation and we will little by little work to get there? And that "there" isn't the only thing that is critical here as the journey is as important if not more important than the destination.

Details take time and many, many mistakes. To reach a final detail — like for instance having a quality backhand stroke in tennis — there are multiple small skills that need to be mastered. Those little skills are also made up of little details like proper footwork, proper grip, proper technique of the skill, etc. These little skills take a long time to get right and a lot of focus on process steps, a lot of persistence, and a lot of success defined as process vs product.

The best coaches demand attention to details, and that attention to details is actually attention to the process steps that make those details great. Details come in many forms. Details come in things like getting to practice on time, getting your laces tied a certain way (John Wooden demanded things like this), everyone paying attention when you are talking/explaining, everyone doing the warm-up the same, and so on and so on. Other details are associated with doing the skill the right way or making this decision at the right time — still okay to demand. But, the critical thing here is the way in which you demand attention to details.

Provide your athletes with an opportunity to continue to *reach* your *expectations* of detail by getting them there little by little until the detail is actually all of the process steps that you have worked on. Playing a perfect game is 100 percent impossible, as is swimming a perfect race, running a perfect race, dancing a perfect routine — all impossible. But, if a coach were to continue to set very high expectations (such that your players could reach them daily), provide players ample opportunities to reach those expectations in order to become better at the small steps it takes to become great at what they do, then the likelihood of reaching that detail is possible. The more you hammer home those small details over and over and over again, then the journey eventually becomes the destination as the skills and choices that you are embedding in your sessions daily become the detailed destination to which you are striving.

This is true for both the pro and the youth athlete as it's all about you and what you are asking for in terms of details. For young ones it can be about the detail of focusing for an entire 30-second explanation, or the detail to do the exercise right, and when they do it, they are rewarded and when they don't, the coach provides appropriate feedback such that they learn what needs to improve in order to do it more right next time. For the pro it is much easier as the margin for error goes way down and details such as man marking, free-throw shooting, running a certain play at a certain time are critical. But an approach to details is key for success at any age, it just depends on what you are asking for.

Here are a few questions to ask yourself when considering how to think about implementing details in an environment:

- Are the details you are asking your players to reach attainable?

- Can the details be broken down further into smaller details that you could teach and ensure improvement on?

- What are you doing when they aren't reaching the details? Are you giving assistance to improve or just throwing your hands up in disgust?

- Are your details the right details? Meaning do you need some changing as perhaps the game has advanced or what you're asking needs some changing?

- Are your daily preparations detailed?

- Are you being detailed in what you are asking your athletes to accomplish — are there detailed criteria that they can check off their list?

- Are you detailed in how you are helping your athletes become good people?

- Are there days when the details you are asking for are about ensuring they are being detailed about having fun or letting loose?

II. Build Motivation and Confidence

Your environment must begin with expectations, but of course if you have expectations, it is up to you to help your athletes reach those expectations. I have seen many coaches over the years have high expectations and then be befuddled when their athletes cannot reach those expectations. A recent example where this might have occurred was with a recently appointed manager of Manchester United during the 2013-2014 season, David Moyes.

Moyes took over as manager from the legendary Sir Alex Ferguson for the 2013-2014 English Premiere League season. It was said that David Moyes came in with some different methods and ideas that he felt would improve his team and help them reach his, and everyone else's, expectations. He went about setting those expectations in trainings and meetings with the players throughout the season. Unfortunately things did not work out this way as the team finished in seventh in the League (their lowest finish since 1993) and Moyes was fired with three games remaining.

Why weren't things successful? By many accounts the manager did a very poor job of motivating his players to buy in to what he wanted — for various reasons. There were stories of player discontent/disagreements and a general lack of desire to perform for the manager. This led to some historic defeats at Old Trafford (their stadium) as they lost to teams that they hadn't lost to — ever! These defeats not only left them wanting for motivation but of course this likely also takes a hit on, you guessed it, their confidence. Of course we weren't in the locker room and are not privy to the daily ins and outs of the environment that was created for the athletes, but if you followed the story of the season closely, this is not a far-reaching premise.

Do not get me wrong, players are also absolutely responsible for their motivation to train and put forth their best effort. But, if a coach can create an environment of expectations and then ensure he or she is also creating an environment that enhances motivation and confidence, then it is also highly likely that players will do some of these things on their own as well. Many would argue in the case of United if Mourinho or Guardiola (two very highly regarded managers who were rumored to have been up for the job) had been appointed that United would not be in the predicament they found themselves in — mostly because those two would have inspired not only expectations but also motivation and confidence as well.

Motivation and confidence are two very important ingredients to have if one wants to have a successful environment. These constructs are deeply rooted in science and, if you have them, even if you fail, you can get back up and get after it again. My background is in sport psychology where, if I could work with my clients to ensure motivation and confidence, I could set them well on their way to better and better performances as time went on. As you see the ideas that I set forth below, understand that I have worked to ensure these in multiple ways with both athletes and coaches. Check out some of the ideas and of course try them out with your athletes to ensure that great environment.

1. Coach the Person, Not the Sport

You coach people, you don't coach a sport. I don't care what sport you are coaching or what level you are coaching or what age you are coaching, it doesn't change. I believe that when you understand the difference between coaching a person and coaching the sport it will forever change the way you present information to your athletes. More importantly, it will have a profound impact on how motivated your athletes are to perform.

When former U.S. Men's National Team Coach Bob Bradley took over the job of coaching the Egyptian National Team he came into a seemingly precarious situation; not only because of the team's desire to qualify for their first World Cup since 1990, but also because the country was in the midst of a massive political and social revolution. Bob Bradley was appointed September 14, 2011. It was a notable hire, given that he was an American, but more importantly because he was an American in a place that was fraught with turmoil, and in a region that is at best wary of Americans and, at worst, massively untrusting. In addition, he took over this position at a time when Egypt was essentially fighting against itself, both with words and with violence. The uncertainty and difficulty was ratcheted up even further, and brought closer to the soccer world, when 79 people were killed at Port Said, a soccer stadium in Egypt, when local fans (and apparently allegedly aided by police who looked the other way) attacked visiting fans. This, among other things, led to a temporary stoppage of play for the league and, of course, made Bradley's job that much more difficult.

So — there is an American manager in a country full of turmoil with a domestic league that isn't allowing its players to play (thus not giving them any advantage as they looked to qualify in games against other countries whose players were playing). Many would not have blamed Coach Bradley and his wife if they had packed up and left simply for safety's sake. What did he do? He coached his people and his sport.

There are countless stories, including a wonderfully produced documentary, about Coach Bradley and his focus on his players as people (and to be fair, the people of Egypt as a whole). He appeared to approach the job with an understanding of how important the sport and World Cup qualification were to the people in the country. He took up residence in the heart of the city (he could have lived in mainland Europe and commuted), and spent countless evenings with his players getting to know his players and their families. In as poignant a gesture as one could possibly make, he chose to march in the city on the day after the Port Said tragedy, when anxiety in the city was high and getting out of Cairo could have been forgiven. Might this show the men that he cared for them as people as opposed to just athletes? How motivated do you think they were to play for Coach Bradley?

Coach Bradley was said to have created and run practice sessions, gave team talks, shouted in games, ensured expectations, and demanded details and accountability, just like any coach would. But, because of his actions it is highly probable that his players knew he was coaching them as people, not just as athletes. He had taken time to get to know them and as a result when these demands were being made they were being made in their best interest and in the best interests of the team, of the people. To do this anywhere is an accomplishment, to do it under those circumstances was extremely difficult and took a great human being who cared a great deal about his athletes as people.

If you want to create a great environment that motivates, yes, set expectations; but help your players get there by treating them as people on their way to becoming athletes. You don't need to be in dire circumstances to think that this makes a difference. It makes a difference anywhere and at any age. Players will see that you are concerned about who they are as people, that you are interested in their "them" and what they want and what they are experiencing. When people know this they are more motivated to perform for you and with you. They will work harder in your sessions, they will more likely do what you are asking of them for the team and they will sacrifice for the greater good, as you have for them.

Building this rapport takes time and effort, and I assure you it's worth it. It'll help you create this great environment and will help you get your message across as you will have receptive ears. Here are a few ideas for you to consider as you undertake the idea of coaching a person vs an athlete.

Take time to chat: I will hit this again in management, but it is critical that you chat them up about who their families are (or moms and dads of little ones) and what they are up to.

Take time to listen: Again this will be hit later, but when they tell you about something, hear it and remember it. Then bring it up again next time you chat.

Talk with them vs at them: Be sure that when you are addressing the group that you include them in your message. Let them feel, through questions, tone and eye catches, that they are part of the plan and that they have input.

Work to understand their goals and what they want: In the end we want them to be motivated to perform. To get them to do this it is helpful that you understand what they want and where they want to go.

Criticize the act, not the actor: Sometimes athletes need to know that the choice they made was one that could have been better. There is nothing wrong with helping someone get better and calling something out that wasn't good enough. But the best way to do is not to say you weren't good enough or you this or that but rather that could have been better or that wasn't good enough. This puts attention on the action vs the person and makes it less personal.

Build a relationship: Relationships take time and real effort. When you are working with your players remember that they will be more motivated when you are seeking to make it an "us" and a "we" vs an "I" or a "you" focus. Really work to get to know them as people as you create your great environment.

2. Build Trust

Coaching athletes as people is critical and is a precursor to this next component as you create a great, motivating environment — that of building trust. Moving athletes along a continuum is rarely, if ever, a smooth process. With bumps come questions and with questions comes possible doubt. If you can build trust within a group you can weather a lot of storms and maintain high motivation as they understand you have the best interest of the individual and the group as a whole in mind.

When I am preparing coaches of young players I use a phrase that hopefully paints a picture of trust. I say when kids know you love them and that they can trust you, then you can get a lot done, and that is a huge responsibility. When I say this what I am saying to these future coaches is 1) it is critical to build trust, but 2) it is critical that you use this trust to build them up as people and as athletes not use it to tear them down or put them in a place where that trust has been misused.

When young athletes trust what you are teaching them, you can ask a lot of them in sessions by asking them to work hard(er), try it this way, try it in games even if you lose. In addition, though, when young athletes trust, there is also great potential for that coach to hurt a young player's feelings with comments that sting very deep given how much they look up to you. As a result this can work to motivate and assist in building confidence OR rip it apart — a big responsibility, no? I believe it is similar with older players but slightly different.

When older athletes understand that they can trust you there is a willingness for them to put themselves fully out there every day, physiologically as well as mentally. The older athletes (club, high school, college or pro) are investing their time and themselves in this joint venture. When you as a coach have taken the time to treat them as people and earn their buy-in, their investment, their output toward the goal and eventually their trust, there is an intrinsic desire to work harder because they are doing it with you, not for you. This notion of doing it with vs for is actually a key ingredient when it comes to building intrinsic motivation as you are doing it as a group vs solo (always better). And, in the end, when an athlete trusts in you and the process they will work harder, run longer and essentially do anything you ask. Why wouldn't they trust you, their guide, on this journey!

Building trust takes time but more importantly it takes you giving them a sense of who you are as a person. It may or may not be obvious that you care about who they are and what they are doing (some of us are better at this than others), but it is critical that they get to see it in glimpses. More importantly, they need to see that you are taking time to do stuff that shows your personal investment to the cause and them. Think of Coach Bradley marching on the streets — might that cause you as a player to think about trusting fully in that coach?

Whatever you do to build trust with your athletes, work to be honest with your players in your dealings with them. Players like to know where they stand in the pecking order and with you overall. Not communicating these things to the player is risky as they are left to guess about your thoughts and feelings. Being a "Man Manager" (discussed later in the book) means being honest, and sometimes that honesty stings, so be smart about how and when you present information.

Trust takes time. But with trust comes a motivated athlete. Work to build that trust and you will see the impact it'll have on your environment.

3. Build Their Motivation From Within

Do athletes win championships by being driven to perform or by driving themselves? Meaning, if you have a collection of athletes who are self-motivated or those that need to be motivated by something or someone else, which ones are likely to take that next step into greatness? Athletes who are self-motivated will persist in the face of failure, enjoy their sport experience, have less anxiety, and overall perform at a higher level when push comes to shove. If you as a coach can set up an environment where your athletes are intrinsically motivated to perform and prepare vs extrinsically motivated to perform, they will persist and pay attention to those details more often and, as a result, will reach toward the expectations that you are setting.

Many athletic environments have those obvious, built-in motivating factors. Things such as we want to make the playoffs or beat that team or finish in the top half of the bracket, are not inherently bad motivating factors. Alongside these "other" rewards is oftentimes the *someone* referred to above — the coach shouting that you need to do this and you need to do that. These are extrinsic motivators, as they refer to the performance of an activity in order to attain some benefit as a result of participation. When people are externally motivated they participate in an activity because it is a means to some end, perhaps a trophy or money, rather than for the sake of participation in the activity itself. Now, of course, this is sometimes a good thing.

Athletes sometimes need someone or something to get them going. They need things to strive for and being motivated by the attainment of these "things" is often very helpful. These incentives — both the coach's voice and the reward at the end — can serve to spark an interest or desire that wouldn't otherwise have been there. But at times, and in time, these can be detrimental, as what if the athletes fall short or tire of the pursuit of these external motivators? What if they have had it with pleasing you as a coach and what you want? Or what if they reach these incentives over and over — will they still be hungry to be successful?

If athletes are primarily motivated by extrinsic means, when the pressure and heat is on, or when they have exhausted and reached or fallen short of these extrinsic motivators, there are a host of negative things that can happen. They will enjoy their sport experience less, work less hard, persist less, experience higher stress levels and more often than not, disengage or quit. Yes, some athletes will be fine, as they will continue to win, beat other people, and get rewards, but many will not, and what of them? Wouldn't we want to ensure that all of our athletes were pursuing their daily endeavors because they wanted to vs because they were told to?

As I said above, the daily environment must be made up of achievable, redefined success criteria that allow the athlete the opportunity to experience success frequently. The environment you create can enhance the likelihood that they pursue these criteria because they want to vs because they have to. The environment that you create can enhance their intrinsic motivation.

Intrinsic motivation refers to performing an activity for the sake of the activity itself. When an individual is intrinsically motivated, he or she is involved in the activity purely for the satisfaction or joy of the activity or to learn something or improve. When athletes love what they are doing they are more likely to do more of it, do it with attention to details and persist at it when things are tough. So the trick is, how do we get them to want to do it on their own? The truth is, we can't. But, if we create the right environment that focuses on some important variables, we most surely can create a place where we are fostering their intrinsic motivation.

The environment you create must include times where you are building their intrinsic motivation to participate. There are actually specific needs in athletes (and everyone for that matter) that, when met, lead to more intrinsic desires to participate. The more a coach focuses on building these essential needs that athletes have, the more the athlete will participate in the activity because they want to vs because they are told to. They will participate for intrinsic reasons, and as a result, get all the benefits of this internal desire. These three needs are competence, choice and feeling a part of the group.

Competence

Competence refers to the idea that one feels like they know about and are good at what it is that they are doing. The goal of the coach, if he or she is to improve intrinsic motivation, is to ensure the athlete feels that he or she is good at, or getting good at, whatever it is he or she is doing. Think about it, how motivated are you to engage in activity if you feel like you are good at it or are getting better at it — likely very — as opposed to feeling like you aren't good at it, and have no chance at being good at it? Creating an environment that improves your athletes' perceptions (or actual knowledge) of how good they are at items in your sessions will increase their internal desire to participate, and as a result they will push harder for the cause.

The critical piece here is that, remember, you are setting the success criteria for ensuring self-referenced success criteria and improvement and, as a result, how athletes can view their competence. When athletes put themselves out there in your sessions as you are asking them to, they will struggle to hit a target at some point. If you are in their ear over and over about this is how we define success, look at how you are improving, and if you aren't satisfied how can you work to improve — you are impacting how competent they feel they are at the task. Feeling competent sometimes involves failures — and that's okay.

Two steps forward, one step back, still shows improvement. Call their attention to actual data so that they can see how they are improving. Make it a gradual sense of how good they feel they are getting. This slow process of them realizing they are improving is a great motivator and is actually the number one way to build confidence as well (discussed later).

Choice

Choice refers to how much say one feels one has in one's development or sport involvement. When people feel like they have some choice in what they are doing, they feel more in control. This control provides anyone, and specifically here the athlete, with some much-needed personal input into perhaps what, when, how long, etc.

they are doing something. In essence what we are talking about here is that if the athlete feels like he or she has some choice in his or her sport, then this will impact the athlete's intrinsic motivation.

Again, think rationally here and recall the Google story. Google employees are given 20 percent of their time to work on projects they care about and are interested in. This free play results in some serious creativity and quality inventions. More importantly though, is this provides some choice, and with that choice Google is making happy employees who are more motivated. When people are provided some measure of freedom and flexibility in their work they are more productive — not only in that 20 percent but in the rest of the 80 percent that they will give back to you.

But what sort of choice and how much choice is appropriate? Listen, you can't let the inmates run the asylum, but to provide opportunities for choice is critical. When you are doing some exercises in training if you sometimes ask your athletes what the right thing to do vs tell them what to do, this provides some choice, even it is an answer that you wanted them to give, they gave it. This is a good one and can be used all the time as you may have what you want for them anyway (training times, time left in an exercise, teams in an exercise, day off, etc.) but if you toss it out to them, and they choose, even if you were going to make the choice anyway, it's very motivating.

Sometimes the perception of choice is all they need. Give them some freedom in what is going on, be creative in how it fits in with your master plan. As they get this choice it has a major impact on their internal desire to participate and perform.

Part of the Group

Feeling part of the group is just that: how much does the person feel like he or she is part of the group? Group cohesion in sports is huge. When you create an environment where athletes feel part of the group, then they will work their tails off, because they want to, for the good of themselves, the group and you. What is interesting here is that, yes, make them feel a part of the team group, but also make them part of your group.

Normally, part of the group refers to how related the athlete feels to the group that they are involved with in the sport (their team), and it does. But there is another place where we can impact their intrinsic motivation through "feeling part of the group," namely that group of two, you and the athlete. It would stand to reason that if the athlete felt part of your group, if he or she were able to feel that you were on their team, in their corner, part of this quest for them to improve, this would also impact their intrinsic motivation.

Recall from above where I say coach the player not the athlete; this is the beginning of establishing that relationship with the player. Show interest in them: like employees at Google, can you provide services that improve the person (as a person and an athlete) and make them feel a part of your group? Are you taking time to impact them daily and making them feel that you are part of their growth and life goals? If you are, you are establishing this small group and as a result impacting their intrinsic motivation.

Are you ensuring the group (team) by ensuring each individual feels a part of that group? Group cohesion is huge. How many times have we seen a lesser quality team roll to a championship because the team cohesion and togetherness is so strong? In most of those examples, every member of the team has a role and every member is fighting for each other, because they want to, not because they have to. Sometimes players take it upon themselves to establish this cohesion, but many times it is the coach who plays a part in establishing an environment where the individual feels part of the group.

When coaches set the tone that everyone is important, it provides a foundation on which group cohesion can be built. The great coaches create an environment whereby all players can get a sense of how they can help the group be successful. From the nonstarter to the best player, and from the injured player to the role player, a coach who creates an environment of involvement is providing these players with information and ideas on how they can help — this is motivating. Some coaches are dismissive of bench players or lesser athletes. This is risky and can really hurt the morale of the team depending on how those people interact with other members of the team. Take time to make all players feel a part of the group; it will lead to higher levels of cohesion and, in the end, more intrinsically motivated players.

4. Build Their Bank of Success – Build Their Confidence

Confidence is a belief in one's self or one's abilities, or full trust, or trustworthiness or reliability of a person or thing. As a coach (or even a fan) we probably all know how important it is to have an athlete who is in "good form" or "looks confident" heading into a big game. Think back to how many times we have seen a confident athlete talk on TV. He usually has had a good performance or some success and usually says the right things and appears as if he has a swagger or way about him that says, "I've got this!"

Perhaps it is tough for us to pinpoint exactly what it is that confident athlete actually looks like, but we certainly recall how they behaved in a practice or in a certain stretch of games where we would have described them as confident. They likely had very good performances or sessions. When they did make a mistake they bounced back quickly, and tried harder and harder each time they fell down. They tossed mistakes out as no big deal and they carried themselves as if they could do anything…no matter what.

So question — is this innate? Built? Both?

The research is inconclusive as to whether or not confidence is innate or built. Most will say it is a combination of both. Sure some people appear naturally confident, but how do we know what happened in their lives up to that point that may have had an impact? Perhaps they were in an environment that provided them every opportunity to learn/ do the critical things that ended up enhancing their self-worth and as a result their self-efficacy, which is basically their confidence.

I have worked with a lot of athletes — from youth to professionals — so I have seen my fair share of "confident" and "not confident" athletes. I have also been exposed to a lot of the research that talks about key sources of self-efficacy that are basically the building blocks of confidence. And my two cents is that it can absolutely be built and I'll give you a few ways for how to do this with and for your athletes. If some of you are still skeptical, let's look at it in a slightly different way.

Can you take someone's confidence away? How many times have we ourselves felt great going in to something only for results to not go our way and suddenly doubt creeps into our minds? Suddenly someone that we trust says to us, "What are you doing?, What was that?, That is what you are going to do? That is awful!" Right then and there your confidence, as well as possible motivation, persistence and desire to participate, is gone.

So why start by ripping it apart first? Well, because my guess is that you can all likely recall an incident when a person that was in charge of your development, or just someone whose opinion you valued, broke your heart in two. Perhaps that person said something to you, or shook their head or did something when perhaps you put yourself out there on the limb and reached. And they knocked you right down, impacting your feelings and approach to what you were doing at the time. He broke more than your heart — he broke your spirit and your confidence, but there is good news. If it can be torn apart it can most certainly be built up.

Building confidence takes an environment that involves driving at a few key variables. Some exceptional researchers in social psychology as well as sport (namely Bandura and Vealey) have identified a few ways self-confidence is built. Basically what they say is that if you enhance these few things you are building someone's confidence little by little. I will soon talk about these items. But first we need a way for you to think about, in a somewhat concrete way, how an environment can be built little by little using these variables.

Let's think of confidence as a bank account. A bank account can be built little by little until it is, or at least we would like it to be, obviously very full and ready to be utilized! In order for this bank account to build, deposits need to be made. Many times, especially early on in life or even with young college or pro players, others (like parents, coaches or peers) are depositing confidence-building comments or experiences into this account. They do it little by little (penny by penny) in a way that doesn't appear to be building up. But over time and after multiple deposits that bank account is noticeably built up as the pennies have turned into dollars, and the dollars have turned into hundreds of dollars. Just like confidence, which is hard to gauge, the athlete doesn't notice that these tiny deposits have built up. But in time every penny adds up, and over time, so does real confidence.

It is on you the coach to create this environment that makes calculated deposits into athletes' accounts. As you help them along this continuum they will gain greater and greater confidence and, in time, players are able to make their own deposits. They understand how their bank account works and they begin to supply some of their own confidence deposits, because they are working hard and smart, and they know how to do this. I would say at this point that you are their financial advisor of sorts. Helping them deposit, and perhaps guiding them ever so slightly into some investment opportunities, putting some of their hard-earned money in various areas in order to continue to help them build, and manage, their bank of success.

Hopefully you see that confidence is built over time and through an environment that you create. Below are three key variables that will allow you to build their bank of success.

Previous Successes – Build Them Up

The number one way that confidence is built is through previous successes. That is to say, the more an athlete experiences accomplishments the more they make deposits into that account and the more confidence they build up. These successes can be many things, both big and small. What is key to remember here is that recall you have redefined how they view success and as a result you actually control what the success is and how they can hit it — as you've defined it!

Recall that the idea is to define success in process and self-referenced terms (get better, work hard, try hard, improve, relative to them) vs product terms (win or lose or be better than someone else). Wins and beating others will happen, and you can use those as well, but sometimes these are few and far between and based on a lot of different factors. These process, self-referenced previous successes build on each other and serve to deposit multiple times into that account in order to build and strengthen confidence.

Take time to create that environment that makes deposits based on previous successes. You will find that as you do this the athletes will, yes, become more confident, but also more motivated and more apt to go after a number of the other things mentioned in the book up to now.

Verbal Persuasion – Make Deposits Via A Trusted Source

So, how are deposits made and why do they make a difference? Deposits are made via you the coach. It is your words and actions of encouragement and comments to help them change and improve that help build an athlete's confidence. This works because you have established trust with the athlete and he or she believes, and internalizes, what you say.

The trust that you worked to establish is critical as you "verbally persuade" them that what they are doing is helping to make them successful. Research in the area of confidence in athletes points to the fact that when athletes trust the source that is giving them feedback, they believe it, and as they believe, it actually builds the confidence. Again, think back to that very important, trusted person who gave you words of encouragement; did it make a deposit? No doubt, yes. This is the same thing. The more you as a coach create an environment that honestly and sincerely makes those deposits with and for an athlete, you are building his or her bank of success and, with it, all of the motivating factors to get done what you and the athlete need to get done.

One thing to be aware of is giving too much or not sincere verbal persuasion. Athletes usually get a sense when a coach is being insincere. In no way are we saying that there must be constant verbal persuasion, but intelligently placed words do indeed build confidence.

Mental and Physical Preparation

When you are creating this environment, be sure to let athletes see and understand that they are becoming more mentally and physically prepared. When an athlete feels mentally and physically prepared he or she feels more confident. So what exactly is mental and physical preparation?

Athletes are mentally prepared when they know they are ready to face the challenges that they will face. The difference between athletes that think they are prepared vs know they are prepared is completely different. Your role in this process is to provide opportunities for athletes to gain this knowledge. This knowledge includes things like:

- Goal setting and a gradual striving and reaching of goals.

- Giving the athlete chances to work on and improve his or her concentration in critical situations (penalty kicks, free throws, passing routes, etc.).

- Giving the athlete chances to engage in multiple problem-solving situations and successfully choosing correctly more often than not.

- Multiple opportunities to feel stress and work through that stress to ensure that it is good stress and not bad stress.

The more chances you create an environment that allows players to feel mentally prepared the more it will positively impact their confidence. Making these deposits takes time and it takes you calling these things to their attention. You must sometimes help the athlete make these connections. As they do they will see that they are more mentally strong, and as a result, more confident.

An athlete is physically prepared when he or she knows they have put in that work to be great. This is an easy one for athletes to see, yet it makes a big difference. When athletes know that they have done everything they can do to prepare, it is a confidence builder. When they can reflect on all of those days of hard work, sprints, laps, long training days, etc., and you remind them, they will see, feel it, know it and, voila, deposit! These deposits make a big difference in time and act as huge motivators as well as confidence builders, because the athletes know that they have put in the work to be great.

III. Foster Thinking and Problem Solving

The best athletes in the world today are the ones who can solve problems and apply these solutions in critical situations. As you look at the world's greats — Rafael Nadal, Andrés Iniesta, Kevin Durant, Sydney Crosby and many more — they make choices in games or competitions that help them or their teams perform well. These athletes are superb athletes, but they are also extremely intelligent athletes who can make choices, under duress, in order to have great performances and positively affect those around them.

Is it coached or innate? As with anything there is, of course, some innateness to it. But an environment rich in opportunities to think and problem solve can simply serve to improve the ability to think and problem solve in games. So, how do they get great and what does problem solving mean?

Problems that present themselves are different for different sports. A simple to understand and common starting spot for all of us is a classroom. Students in today's world can find answers to questions at a moment's notice, such as who was this person, what is the answer to this math problem, what happened in such and such war? These answers are easily found on the Internet, and that's a good thing. But what about one's ability to perhaps determine why that person was the way they were? What about why and when one would learn to perform a certain math problem or perhaps why a particular war was waged, what precipitated it and what could have prevented it? These are questions that take critical thinking and problem-solving skills and an environment that enhances those skills.

One of the best books I have read in a long time is a book by Dr. Derek Cabrera entitled *Thinking at Every Desk*. Dr. Cabrera asserts that there are far too few opportunities in schools for our students to think, and that he found out about this once he had the "smartest" kids in the country in his Harvard classroom. He discusses that he quickly realized that they could recall with great accuracy, that they had mastered learning, but that they had a fundamental inability to critically think and analyze. In his book he posits that every person is born with the desire and faculties to be able to problem solve, but that we educate him or her out of it instead of into it. He asserts that if we set up our environment correctly that we can create a foundation for everyone to be able to problem solve.

Critical to Dr. Cabrera's DSRP method for building thinking skills are two premises: 1) that people build knowledge, and 2) that the knowledge that they build is ever changing. He asserts, and involves in his teaching method, that, yes, people need a base of information. For him the base is a) a mind-set and b) root lists. For a classroom it is a) an expectation of learning and b) the "basics." For your coaching sessions they are a) expectations and b) learning the basics (proper techniques and patterns).[8]

The critical step for someone creating an environment of thinking and problem solving is the guiding questions that ask a person to think about how and when to use these skills. This is in essence the Socratic method of teaching where a learner would have this mind-set and foundational skills and then be asked "How do you think you can use this or that?" Not randomly but with an outcome that the teacher/coach could guide them along a continuum to encourage thinking and problem solving.

I would highly encourage anyone to read Cabrera's book and think how they may be able to apply it to their sport or classroom environment. For me, this book has helped to solidify some of the ways I view elite coaches and how I assist emerging coaches become good at helping their athletes think. I have for years heard coaches at the highest level say that our athletes need to be able to think and problem solve — but they don't really talk about how to do this. How do you structure your practices? What do you say? When do you say it?

Having an environment that fosters these things is CRITICAL as we enter this next phase of human kind. The best jobs in the world take thinkers (that have a quality mind-set and a foundation of knowledge), and the best teams in the world are thinking teams with thinking athletes (who have the right mind-set and an arsenal of skills and abilities). Any person at any age can learn to think. Here are a few ways for you to establish an environment that fosters thinking and problem solving:

1. Establish That Mind-Set of Expectations and Foundations For Player Success

Establishing the expectations that we spoke of earlier is critical to how a player will engage in his or her thinking process. When an athlete has these expectations that you have set as the standard for your environment, what he or she has is a starting point, a lens of sorts, for how to view each and every learning context in which they engage. An athlete will automatically start with a mind-set of, okay, this is what is expected of me so I will engage in the day's activity with purpose and intent. Setting this mind-set then ensures that the athlete is "dialing in" to the day and cognitively engaging his or her entire body and mind in to what is going on.

I have seen this with six-year-olds and with twenty-six-year-olds, and the results are exactly the same (I'm not kidding): engaged, thought-filled, participants. The six-year-olds are simply asked to be engaged in the day and "dial in" by running and freezing and the coach giving them "atta-boys" and a "can you try it this way?" The kids are being asked to engage in the day in a positive and age-appropriate way, thus setting the stage for the day's activities and the thinking that will be involved. The adults are similar but take more communication and prodding and asking and demanding as they enter their sport experience for the day. But the result, if managed correctly, is that they are ready to engage in the day, if the expectations of engagement are set and demanded early. We covered a bit of this above and will cover a lot more of it in the management section, as managing your athletes in the beginning of a session is key to establishing an environment.

Ensuring athletes have a foundation is also critical to being able to ask them to think in your environment. If players do not have a foundation of "fundamentals" (see John Wooden, Coach K, Pat Summit, Nick Saban or any successful youth coach for the importance of these fundamentals), they do not have a starting place from which to think. Arming athletes with fundamentals like simple techniques, skills and abilities is that starting place, that foundation. From this starting place (which is similar to the D in Dr. Cabrera's DSRP theory and/or the root list in his DSRP methods explanation from above) our athletes have a solid foundation from which to begin solving problems. If people have more skills and abilities, then they can begin to make more connections (like pass here or there, run here or there, run this type of play or offense, etc.). When athletes can make more connections they can problem solve more and learn to do that in games and critical situations.

2. Ask Them To Problem Solve vs Tell Them What To Do

Sometimes the answer to the problem that we are posing to our athletes in training is obvious to us, and we could easily give them the solution. Let it go, ask them to problem solve vs give them the answers. I have seen the value of this in the classroom.

When you are working with students, from age six to age twenty-six, there is a moment when you ask a question that you can see the student searching for the answer. Yes, you can give them the answer in that moment and as a result they will have that nugget. Or, you can lead them along that path in such a way as to allow them the opportunity to answer the question. When students get that answer on their own, make that connection as it were, there is this ah-ha moment that is sometimes almost giddy for them. They see that they got the answer, and that they did it and it's powerful. If that moment can be created time and time again, it provides them with an opportunity to make their own connection, which leads to a more powerful image in the mind because it is from their context and, as a result, it also leads to more confidence.

Creating an environment that asks athletes to solve problems in trainings as opposed to always giving them the answers creates rich learning opportunities, provides the learner with an opportunity to make his or her own connections and builds confidence. It's "rich" because it's a multidimensional way of doing business, meaning there is an opportunity to listen, think, make mistakes, and overall engage in the process of learning vs the product of learning. This "multidimensionality" means that the sessions are more like games, in that they are full of different situations and opportunities to solve problems and be successful, or not. Games are never predictable and, as a result, require athletes that can function in an unpredictable environment. Creating sessions with this rich, multidimensional environment at the heart of it prepares them for this type of game situation.

Creating an environment that asks athletes to solve problems in trainings provides them with an opportunity to make their own connections. When an athlete makes his or her own connections he or she is making new meaning out of what they are learning. This is similar to what is known as scaffolding, which is what it sounds like, meaning stacked on each other. In this case it is a bit different as they aren't just stacked on each other, but they do rely on each other to make a new meaning.

Take, for example, an athlete learning how to do a give and go in basketball or soccer. The athlete must first learn how to pass a ball (foundation). Then the athlete must learn to give it to a teammate, at the right time. This takes time and repetition and multiple attempts all by itself. Now the athlete must learn to go after the *give* in order that the other player may be able to play that ball to him after he *goes*. This new meaning has been arrived at after trial upon trial upon trial...and error upon error and you get my point. The athlete, if given the right environment and cues (we will talk more about this in the content area), can learn. Through scaffolding the athlete can make these connections. Once these connections are made they are made in the learner's context and as a result have made a bigger impact on their learning than they would have if you just told them.

Finally, creating an environment that asks athletes to solve problems builds confidence. As touched on previously the number one confidence builder is that one has done it before. When an athlete comes to a conclusion on his or her own, they naturally make a deposit. The more they can make their own deposits, by coming to their own conclusions, the more they can continue to fill their bank account.

Following are a few suggestions for you to create that problem-solving environment.

Ask questions and help them get answers: I mentioned the "Socratic Method" above. Basically it is the idea that you can really spur a learner, and in this case an athlete, to come to his or her own conclusions by asking the athlete open-ended questions that can hopefully help him or her get to the answer. Questions such as: What may have been a good way for him to get to goal? Or, what would have been a good choice for that player to make in that situation? This gets that brain working and can lead to those rich answers in their context.

Leave questions open-ended to keep all on toes: I mentioned above to keep questions open-ended. One of the reasons for this is because it stimulates the person toward a solution, provided you are helping them make connections if they can't get it. But I also mean to not slap a name on the question right away. Meaning, don't say, "Tom, what do you think?" But rather say, "What do you all think about that?" The first way basically says to everyone, I am asking Tom so everyone else go ahead and shut down. But the second way ensures that all are potential recipients of the question, thus ensuring everyone is on their toes, so to speak.

When you stop, don't give answers — ask group and ensure they are ALL thinking: When you stop the group the tendency is for you to give that answer and say this is the way it should be done. Yes, sometimes you may need to do that. But, more often than not ensure that when you stop the session to make a point — see if you can start it with a question instead of an answer. Then as it goes forward see if you can have the athlete paint that picture on the field or court. Make sure the athletes can see it from their perspective and check for understanding.

Check for understanding: Some learners are very visual and need you to check to see if they got it. Check for understanding by having the players walk through the point you were trying to make. Remember, we are wanting to create an environment where thinking takes place, and many people think in pictures not words. So check for understanding by "painting the picture" so to speak, and moving the pieces into the spots such that all athletes can see what it is you were asking them to think about.

3. Ensure Opportunities For Failure As They Think

We spoke about failures above, but it bears repeating here; providing an environment for athletes to think and fail is fantastic. When you ask an athlete to think, there is a tremendous amount of opportunity for the athlete to succeed but also fail. But as we said above, failure and success, when handled correctly, are important and equally valuable.

My mom was a tremendous foreign language teacher for many reasons, but one was her sense of the value of a red pen. I remember my mom talking to me about how upset she was that a school that she happened to be teaching in was concerned that when kids received red pen marks all over papers and exams, it was hurting their self-esteem. That the red pen marks were saying to the kids that they had failed, and calling attention to this failure with a traditional red pen was bad — as if they failed, and attention was called to it, then they were a failure.

My mom was upset about this, as she valued being able to say to a student in an up front and honest way, that the effort was a great try but it needs work; and if we want to be able to communicate with someone in another language, let's approach it a different way. Her premise was, of course, that the red pen was actually good, as yes of course a red pen had traditionally been used to simply mark up stuff, but she used it properly, to provide assistance and much-needed feedback. Her real reason was, look, the world will ask you to communicate using this completely foreign language to you, and it's not easy to put yourself out there as you could get very lost or very taken advantage of and my so-called harsh "red pen" is actually a helper, not a hinderer, and will prepare you for life. That the red pen mark wasn't inherently bad, as everyone fails and fails often, and that it was just a way to say hey, it needs fixing, let's fix it up and get after it again.

My mom speaks five languages and taught languages in middle and high school. She understood the value of creating an environment where her students were expected to think and maneuver their way around the language they were learning in order to be able to use it to communicate. When she handed papers and assignments back, yes, she used a red pen, but she used it for good instead of evil! She gave corrective feedback and encouraged her students to try it different ways. Moreover, she encouraged her students to try different things with their newfound language abilities (or lack thereof), encouraging them to reach further and further out, all with a red pen!

When athletes are made to think they are often wrong, or not all right, and when they are not all right in games, they get hit with life's red pen. So what! Use your trainings to expose them to life's red pen by asking them to think and when they aren't 100 percent correct, help them get it right. If they are still wrong, which they will be often, let them know to try it another way and see if they can come up with a solution on their own. Sometimes this needs to be done in a very up-front way; do it and remember that the goal is constant improvement, not constant perfection. If they can learn to self-correct, to use their own red pen, then these small failures are all just a part of being better and better.

Bottom line, ensure multiple opportunities for thinking and failing. Yes, let them get it right but have them learn to come to those conclusions, through trial and error, in a safe environment that is in essence a safety net for thinking! Have them continue to reach and reach and over time they will get better and better at solving problems in sessions, and eventually games.

Overall, creating an environment that asks, encourages and teaches players to think and solve problems is not only great for the player but also great for you as a coach. It provides you the coach with an opportunity to challenge your own thinking and ways of doing things in order to get your "ways" and content better and better. No matter what, creating an environment that fosters thinking and problem solving is critical to who you are as a coach and as a result what types of players you will be helping to create and nurture.

The environment you create for athletes will be critical to their development as athletes and people. For me it is the number one thing that great coaches do and that young coaches need to do in order to be successful. I encourage you, an emerging coach, to watch and read about great coaches and see what they do to create an environment that helps their athletes be great. More importantly if you as a young coach can get around a great youth or young adult coach — do it so you can see an environment taking shape, which is a thing of beauty.

Now we are heading into the Management section. As you read it, do not forget the previous sections of Presence and Environment. This method of coaching is one that builds on itself. You will see that I will refer back to and reuse items I have already discussed. I encourage you, as you continue to read, to read back what you have previously read if, for instance I am talking about the value of thinking or failures, etc., take time to review what we have previously discussed.

Chapter 5

Management

The head of a professional baseball or soccer team (apart from in America) is called a manager, as is the head of a company. Actually, manager is a fairly logical term to use when you think about the goals of each of the entities stated above, which is to manage the people and direction of that group. In fact, a closer look reveals a bit more about why the terms are used as well as what makes a good manager a good manager, regardless of profession.

In baseball, the manager is responsible for everything from selecting players for positions on game day to overall leadership of a team. The manager makes a number of in-game decisions such as when to change pitchers, how to and when to give a player a rest on game day, to perhaps even helping to select a certain pitch to throw at a certain batter. More importantly, though, the best baseball managers manage personalities.

Many times these teams are made up of big personalities (think Joe Torre and the big-name New York Yankee teams of the early 2000s). It is the responsibility of the manager to talk with, know and work with these athletes — both on and off the field. The manager needs to know about what might be impacting the daily life of a player, and perhaps even work through some daily life issues, in order help that player focus on game day. The manager will also frequently have staff (assistant coaches and backroom for example) that he needs to manage so that they can work with each of the players, again both on and off the field. The bottom line is that the best managers in baseball are good at making the game day/ time decisions as well as managing relationships with their players in order that they are successful on game day.

Soccer managers throughout the world function in a similar capacity as baseball managers. Many soccer managers run day-to-day sessions with their players, as well as choose and lay out how they will play an opponent on game day and who will play where in that game. But the best managers in soccer manage people and situations in order for their team to be successful.

If you do an Internet search for any good manager in world football (soccer) — Pep Guardiola, Philip (Felipe) Scolari, Roberto Martinez — they appear to have a sensational understanding of the game and can "coach," but more importantly they are fantastic managers of people. These managers have a knack for being able to get the most out of the players they select because they ensure that they talk with the athletes in order to motivate, understand, help, teach and manage. In addition, these managers take the time to ensure that every detail is sorted out, from detailed training sessions to when players arrive in camp or at games to what they will eat to where they will spend the night before a game. Similar to baseball, these managers have additional staff that will help them with these tasks, but of course it falls on them to manage these people as well. The goal of the manager, then, is to ensure his players are prepared for game day in order that they may be successful.

Let's switch gears a bit here and talk about the role of a manager in a business or company. Get a picture of any business, McDonalds, IKEA, Foot Locker or even Dunder Mifflin, each of these managers are responsible for day-to-day activities, placing orders for product, placing employees in correct positions, ensuring training for new employees, etc. But the best managers not only do the day-to-day duties very well, ensuring a smooth daily work environment and business, but they also manage the employees and those relationships extremely well.

In fact, a closer look at quality managers reveals that managing people is as important as managing day-to-day activities. Alan Murray, a journalist and economist, studied managers in order to see what makes them effective. Mr. Murray came up with five things a great manager does.[9]

1. A great manager sets objectives and goals for the group, and decides what needs to be done in order to reach those goals and objectives.

2. A great manager organizes the group and then divvies up the work into smaller activities. In addition, he or she places people who are good at certain tasks in charge of doing those tasks at the right times.

3. A great manager motivates and communicates. This one is fairly self-explanatory, but a great manager finds ways to ensure his or her staff are motivated to get their work done. He or she also properly communicates with individuals, both about work and about who they are as people.

4. A great manager measures success. In essence, a manager takes stock of what targets have been hit or missed and then goes about making adjustments to ensure these are hit over time.

5. A great manager develops people. Of course, I love this one as this gets at the heart of what I believe a great coach, and in this case a great manager does. They manage people, they do not just manage their business.

As we look at what Mr. Murray indicates are the key things for a manager in business, they are quite similar to what a manager in sport does. They manage situations, day-to-day line ups/tasks, ensuring productivity on the field/in the office, make adjustments on the field/in the office to ensure the group is successful. But, they also manage people. Great coaches are great managers and great managers manage situations and people.

You cannot teach if you cannot manage. Any good coach at any level knows this and goes about managing the minutia. Before we get on to what specific things one can do to manage situations and people, let's deconstruct a great coach/manager. Let's deconstruct Nick Saban, the head coach for the University of Alabama football program.

Love him or hate him, Saban is one of the most successful college football coaches in history. He has coached college and professional football for over 40 years. During that time Coach Saban has won multiple championships including four NCAA national championships, with his latest national championships coming in 2009, 2011, and 2012 with his current team, the Alabama Crimson Tide.

Coach Saban is known for many things, but one of the things he is best known for is his attention to detail and how he manages things in order to ensure that detail gets done. Coach Saban is a respected coach, but also a respected manager of people. He is routinely asked to speak to Fortune 500 companies and their executives about his leadership style and management abilities. Basically, people want to know how he manages situations and people.

One of the things Coach Saban is said to do in order to manage situations and people is institute and execute what he calls "The Process." I recommend that everyone who wants to establish a true process for managing the minutia should read about it however you can, in books or on the Internet).[10] "The Process" is basically a step-by-step plan to ensure success for the people involved. It appears to set forth detailed approaches for players for how they should approach their daily endeavors. Each piece builds on the next so that players are ready to perform. But it's more than just a "do this and do that" list for the players. It also indicates to the staff how situations and players should be managed in order that they can be successful.

"The Process" refers to how situations should be managed with and for the player. Yes, it talks about on-field situations — decisions for certain plays, how to finish (the game, the practice, the fourth quarter, etc.), how to prepare to play against certain teams, etc., and these are critically important. But it talks a lot about how to manage off-the-field situations as well. Coach Saban ensures he is helping the player manage the media, manage off-field distractions, manage what to eat and when, and all of the little situations a college player might find himself in at a young age. Coach Saban is keenly aware that he is managing people in these situations.

Saban appears to understand that he is managing young adults who are still very much emerging into who they can and will become over time. He appears to understand that this takes daily management. Coach Saban is said to meet with the players individually to get to know them as people. He institutes mandatory study sessions, ensures they get to class, talks to them about how to dress for success, what life after college has in store, and so forth. He manages the person, daily and down to the minute.

Really what this appears to be is that Saban isn't just operating a college football program, he is operating and *managing* his own company. Could it be that Coach Saban's company is managed because he 1) sets objectives, 2) organizes the group and places people who are good at certain tasks in charge of doing those tasks at the right times, 3) manages, motivates and communicates, 4) measures success and 5) develops people? My guess is that Mr. Murray would approve of the way Coach Saban is managing his company!

This management is key for any coach at any level in any sport. How and what we do to manage will vary from sport to sport and age to age. I'd like to take the next few pages to run through a few areas that great coaches should consider as they begin to manage their team. You will see that I have organized it for adults and children as there are different needs for each group. My goal is to provide some concrete ideas for the reader to use if they want to improve their managerial skills as a coach.

College/Pro – On the Field
(and things related to the field)

Managing players on the field/court is important. Recall that managing situations and people means getting out in front of a number of items in order to ensure that athletes are on track and motivated as well as confident to perform and be successful. There are multiple things that a coach must consider as he or she prepares for and actually coaches their teams on the day. The majority of these management suggestions are things written for coaches of team sports. I do believe that many of these can be for individual athletes as well, but there are probably a whole host of other items that I am not including for that particular group of people; perhaps I'll save those for an addendum for the book.

Practice: Holding players accountable at practice is a management issue. I mention it above but it bears repeating here, as I have said many times if you cannot manage your athletes at training, how can they learn to perform what you are asking them to perform? So what are we talking about when we say manage your athletes at training?

Managing athletes at trainings encompasses everything from ensuring athletes are concentrating, to ensuring they are learning, and from ensuring they are on time to ensuring they are ready once they arrive. I have seen multiple coaches simply allow their athletes to show up to training and train without holding them accountable for items that will ensure standards are reached and that they are reaching your expectations. Recall from the environment section that we said there must be expectations. The management of this component of this section of the environment is where the rubber meets the road, it's where and how you actually hold them accountable.

Following is a list of things you should ensure you "manage" daily in your practices. Manage it by calling attention to it and communicating with your athlete that these are the expectations and this is what is expected. (FYI, I will address specifics on perhaps how to communicate in the communication section later, thus tying in this as well as the environment.)

- *Players need to be on time:* Everyone's time is valuable. Athletes should treat your sessions with respect and place a high value on yours and their teammates' time. They are functioning adults and, as such, should abide by your rules. If they are late, there is no need to call them out in front of the group but it should be mentioned and there should be a consequence if it is habitual.

- *Players should be focused*: Players cannot learn if they are not focused. Get them to "dial in" to the session by getting their attention with the way you are using your voice or body language. Whatever you do, ensure you manage their attention.

• *Players should have their proper gear on, properly:* If you have a designated training uniform it should be worn and worn properly. If it isn't, then they aren't paying attention to details. It is a small detail, but important.

• *Players need to work to get it right:* Again we discussed this previously but you should absolutely demand that your athletes are striving. If they are not putting the mental energy to work to get it right, they are short-changing the process.

• *Players should be listening:* All players should be engaged in meetings or team talks. No one is above the law or exempt. If a player is tuning out, it is unacceptable.

• *Players should have a good attitude:* Everybody has a bad day, it happens. But it doesn't mean that person who is having a bad day gets to sabotage your session. Ensure the athlete knows you care that he or she is struggling, and perhaps chat with them at some point about it. But others are there to work and you must ensure that that attitude changes in your training to ensure learning and effort stays high for everyone. "Good" doesn't mean they need to be all smiles, but they do have to approach their endeavor with purpose and intent to get something out of the day.

Ensure players know their roles and responsibilities: One of the greatest compliments I have heard bestowed on a coach is that his or her players understand their roles and responsibilities on the field or court. This is absolutely a management issue (see #1 and #2 in Murray's list above) as players need to know what they are responsible for doing at the end of the day.

The very successful Major League Soccer manager of the Houston

Dynamo, Dominic Kinnear, has had this said about him. Many a player who has played with or against Coach Kinnear remarks about how everyone has a role on the field and that those roles are clearly defined for each and every player. He takes time to manage every player and situation to ensure they know what to do where and when. This is very empowering for the players as they not only know what to do but how they will be judged. Whether this is exactly how it happens, I cannot say. But if you watch any of Coach Kinnear's teams they are extremely well disciplined, play in a similar fashion (regardless of personnel), and are successful every year!

My point, make sure players know what to do. When players know their roles and responsibilities in training and more importantly, in games, it is empowering. Take time to manage this minutia, as it will pay dividends over time.

Manage bench players: In a similar vein, make sure that every athlete, even the bench players, are managed. Many coaches do not pay attention to those fringe players who may not be playing all that much. Instead, coaches choose to ignore or not communicate with those players about why they are where they are. But, what happens when you need them? Will they be there to fight for you or the cause?

The best managers of people know that everyone is valuable and can play a part in the "The Process." Bench players need to be managed, they need to be spoken with and brought into the plans of the team. Initially, because it is the right thing to do, as that person is part of the team and as a result should be given the same respect as anyone else. But also because at some point you may need that player to contribute to the group and, if you have managed that person, he or she will likely be there. But if you have ignored that person, then you are simply taking a chance that he or she will be ready when called upon.

Manage the injured athlete: Being injured is a very painful process, both physically and psychologically. When athletes are injured they are in for what sometimes can be a grind physically to get back to good. The other painful part about being injured is that you are removed from the team in order to rehabilitate. When an athlete is removed from the team, there is often a social element that the athlete is lacking and, as a result, there may be lingering doubt or uncomfortableness as he or she rehabilitates.

A good coach must manage the injured athlete by touching base with him or her often and including him or her in the team wherever possible. I have seen good managers do a great job of this. The great manager of people in this situation goes out of his or her way to chat with the athlete, both in the office, in the gym, in the physio room and via text and phone. Just connecting with the injured athlete keeps him or her in the loop and motivated. I have also seen good managers ensure that they continue to invite the player to meetings and trainings whenever possible. It's not always possible to do this, but when a player can be involved in this stuff it is good as, again, it keeps him or her in the loop and motivated.

__Manage group cohesion:__ Groups that are tighter tend to perform at a higher level. Managing the tightness of a group takes a lot of work. Be sure you have players who you can count on to take the pulse of the team. Taking this pulse can help you determine if you have work to do to pull the team together a bit. Take time to build your team's cohesion. Doing team-building activities and getting the team together off of the field can help them on the field.

__Manage goals and progress toward those goals:__ Players need goals for which to strive. Ensuring players understand where they are going and how they will get there is important. Be sure that you set these goals with your players as opposed to for them, and that you take time to evaluate progress on these goals. Also be sure players understand their role in reaching or falling short on these goals. Personal accountability is important and takes time to build.

__Manage the team leaders:__ Most teams have captains and those captains are expected to lead. But do they know how to lead, especially relative to what you expect of a leader? Don't make the mistake of naming a captain and then not managing that captain in terms of what you expect day in and day out.

Captains are basically an extension of you with the players. Some captains will know exactly what to do and when to do it, but some will not. Provide these leaders with an opportunity to get a sense of how you manage people; what you want them to do on the field as a leader and what things you expect them to take care of off of the field as well. Also, when they make errors, which they will, ensure these are learning experiences as well, communicate with them about changes that need to be made, with whom those changes need to be made, and when they need to happen. Be demanding, but manage them so they can help you manage your team.

Manage motivation and confidence: We spoke about this in the environment section, but this is where you get to see if what you are doing is working. Check in with your athletes often to see if you are building trust, internal motivation, their bank of success, and so on. This is critical to their on-field performance as well as to their development as people.

Doing this is as simple as choosing one of those concepts from the environment section and asking them, indirectly, about it. Find out how excited they are to be at trainings or games. Or, ask them how well they understand a certain play or exercise or how they are feeling about their next opponent (competence). These are very important conversations and will give you a lot of information about where that athlete is in terms of his or her motivation and confidence at that time.

Game day: Game days are days that need to be managed. There is a lot going on for the athlete on game day. All the athlete needs to worry about is doing is his or her job — playing the game in the way that you have prepared him or her to do. So, manage the minutia.

Every level of performance carries with it different detailed items that need to be managed. It would be impossible to list all of those things, but things like uniforms are readied, line-up and assignments known, transportation sorted, tickets for friends and families taken care of, media responsibilities are known early, time of warm-up known, are just a few of the things athletes should have done for them or know about as soon as possible. The more these things can be "known about" the fewer surprises there are for the athletes. The fewer surprises, the more control; the more control the less anxiety; and the less anxiety, the better the chance of a smooth and quality performance.

I would also say touch base with the athletes on game day. Chat them up and make them feel comfortable. Some will not want to be bothered, so know that, too. But, many of them enjoy a bit of a chat as they are getting prepared. Remember they are people, and most people like to be communicated with, not just when things are good but when there is serious work to do as well.

My suggestion for new coaches at the college or pro level is to make a list. It sounds silly, but if you can work through a list of things that you want to ensure you manage on game day it will give you a guide and also something to do, as nerves come to all and this may just be a good way to manage you.

College/Pro – Off the Field

Managing players off of the field is where I really want to spend my time in this section. When players and their off-the-field needs are managed well then the athlete can devote more of his or her mind to simply playing the game. I have seen this up close and personal with some of the teams I have worked with at the highest level.

Some teams I have worked with ensured that their athletes were taken care of — ensuring housing, family comforts, contracts done and dusted, and everything you might think of that would make an athlete feel comfortable as he settled into his new team and city. I have also seen teams manage their athletes extremely poorly — basically doing the opposite of the things I say above. In both cases there was a massive impact on performance. Think about it, if an athlete has his or her spouse getting upset with them, or they are getting poor sleep because they are stuck in a hotel room, or they are eating poorly because they are eating out every night because they have no kitchen, it affects performance.

If you as a coach can ensure that you take care of all the little things, then the athlete is left to concentrate on playing (and going to school for those in college). If the coach can minimize off-field distractions by managing the minutia, then the athletes can use more of their resources to do the things that they need to do, perform on the court/field and in the classroom.

Here are a few examples of off-field situations that need to be managed. Some are germane to college, while some are more appropriately suited to professional sports. Either way, these should serve as starting points for you to consider how to help manage your athletes.

Ensure they have a quality place to live: I have heard and seen horror stories about athletes stuck in hotels or on couches for far too many days. When an athlete has a steady place to live, he or she feels settled. When an athlete feels settled, he or she can get down to business — be it a pro team a college team or a college classroom. This is, of course, important to a young, single college or pro athlete as that is just one less thing to think about. But the importance of this to a family cannot be understated.

When a player with a family is relocated, it is not just him or her, it is an entire family. If an entire family is unsettled, then there is a major impact on the parent that is playing. This is a distraction that not only impacts how he or she performs but also how he or she feels about the team that isn't sorting out their housing. Many athletes take this personally and, when it isn't done right, then they feel their anger toward the very club that they are being asked to perform for on a daily basis.

Manage an athlete's housing situation. It is critical and is as important as anything you can do for an athlete. Once this is taken care of, an athlete has a place to go in order to get away from it all and regenerate for what's next.

Ensure families are taken care of (for pros mostly): Along the same lines, make sure that a player's family is taken care of once they arrive. There are a number of things that coaches or clubs simply don't think about. Things like ensuring a good family physician, a school for the kids, a social network for the happenings, etc. Assisting the family with these items is just another example of managing the person and ensuring they are comfortable and settled in order to perform.

Ensure contracts/scholarships done and dusted: Usually when a college player arrives on campus their scholarship and everything that goes with it is understood, but sometimes not. In addition, a player may not know how his or her scholarship works from year to year. The best college coaches leave no ambiguity and ensure their student-athletes know exactly what their scholarship covers and for how long. Athletes appreciate this, and this is just another example of being up front in how you manage a young athlete.

A professional needs to have it be very clear what aspects are covered under his or her contract. You would think this would be cut and dried, and that an agent would take care of this minutia, but it isn't and they frequently don't. And, if these things don't get taken care of, you can have a very disgruntled employee who, like it or not, is looking to you in frustration and perhaps is even blaming you to some extent. So, make it your business to manage this piece. Check into it and make sure he or she is getting what he or she should be getting. It'll show the athlete that you are checking in on them and that he or she is important to you.

Ensure that the student has every opportunity to be successful (college only): This aspect must be managed, and in many big-time college programs is managed by an entire department. My guess is that at Alabama there are a whole host of people at the service of the football program. But, the coach makes it his business to ensure academics are a top priority by having study halls, tutors and academic counselors dedicated to the program and overall having high expectations of success. Managing this piece for college coaches may seem obvious, but it is still worth noting here as managing this is a critical piece to managing a college (and high-level high school) athlete.

Make sure you have good help: In order for a program to run smoothly it needs quality assistants and "back-room" staff. Almost every program out there (college or professional) has a budget for assistant coaches. These coaches really help out with the day-to-day running of any program. But what they also do is help you manage your athletes. Make sure that when you hire an assistant that he or she has different communication qualities than you and can see and get around to athletes differently than you. If you have two of the same personalities, then perhaps you will be duplicating your management efforts, and that's not what you need. He or she should have the same philosophy but should manage people slightly differently to serve as a balance.

Back-room staff refers to medical staff, trainers and other supplemental staff that most college and professional teams have available to assist players. These people are frequently the eyes and ears of your organization as they will see athletes often and frequently in intimate one-on-one situations. These situations leave them with a real opportunity to manage that person within your team. Make sure these people are saying the right things, in the right way, and moving the ship in the direction that you are intending it to go. Equip them with an ability to communicate effectively with the athlete and ensure you talk with them often to see what they may be hearing or doing with the athletes.

__Make sure athletes know how to manage money:__ This one is perhaps best suited for professional teams, but is applicable to college as well. For college athletes perhaps it's helping them manage what little additional money they receive as part of their scholarship allotment. Or perhaps they aren't receiving any money and they have loans that they are taking out to help put themselves through school. Either way, sitting them down to discuss how to manage this money over the course of the year is important. Do not assume they know how to do this, as many of them do not.

Many professionals do not know how to manage their money. In the bigger sports leagues in the United States, the league puts on rookie information sessions with this as one of the topics. But, this is not the case with all of the leagues. Many leagues do not do this for their athletes as they do not have the resources. Take the time to sit with your athletes to assist them in how they might manage their money now and in the future.

__Help athletes manage their down time:__ Many athletes know how to play and train hard but they have no idea what to do the other 20 hours of the day. When young athletes get to college they have all kinds of freedom that they did not have before they arrived. Teaching kids how to manage this time is essential if they are to survive their time in school, not to mention their time in their athletic endeavor.

Professional athletes are not that different, apart from the fact that they have a bit more money to go crazy with during the day. For a professional many times the workday is done by noon, so now what? A player who knows how to manage his or her time finds other things that interest him or her and pursues those interests. Sometimes it's video games, sometimes it's reading, sometimes it's real estate. Whatever it is, it needs to be something that takes minimal energy and ensures that they are not out spending too much money and are not up to shenanigans.

Take the time to talk with athletes about things they can do with their down time. It is important to their (and your) success and very much needed. Don't assume.

Manage players' mental health and behavior: Athletes are not robots, yet we ask them to perform, under pressure, day in and day out and sometimes with very little breaks in between these moments of pressure. My point is athletes face a pressure to perform that is usually more than what the normal person faces. Many times these athletes cope with this stress very well, giving themselves small mental breaks, talking themselves out of difficult situations, and generally dealing with this pressure in stride. But sometimes they do not, and that's okay. It is sometimes up to the coach to manage and help the athlete manage these emotions.

I have seen firsthand what stress can do to athletes in pressure situations, at the youth, college and professional levels. If feelings or stress-related issues are not managed properly, players perform poorly in games, negatively affect their teammates, behave poorly with friends and family, turn to drugs or alcohol, do serious mental or physical damage to themselves, and eventually quit. I have seen all of these things happen firsthand.

Instead of talking about or working through these issues, athletes will oftentimes just look to grind it out as they do not want to talk about stress or pressure with anyone for fear of appearing weak. This is silly and from an era of sport long ago where we asked players to not have feelings or to work through their feelings. We, as coaches and managers, need to provide our athletes with opportunities to work through this stress and potential anxiety with us as a staff or another professional. But sometimes it is up to us as coaches to spot and manage this process, as athletes frequently do not know how to even embark on this change process.

As a coach, help the athlete manage these potential mental and physical issues. This doesn't mean that you walk up to the athlete and say are you stressed out, get help. Be smart and subtle and be a person, not a coach. If you are managing your players, you are talking with them often. Simply monitor their behavior, you will begin to see signs of things that may be going on with the player or his/her family. Ensure that once you see things going awry that there is a culture in place to assist the athlete and ensure he stays mentally healthy. You will see that by managing things like this that your players not only perform better over time but also stay healthy as a person.

Manage the next phase of career opportunities – college or pro:
Athletes aren't athletes forever and, as a result, need to have a skill set and ideas about what's next. College athletes are in a place that, hopefully, is preparing them for a what's next time. This "what's next" includes education, discussions with counselors about job opportunities, and likely opportunities for internships and other things that can help with improving and implementing their skill sets. I would also say, though, that discussion with you the coach becomes pretty important here as well as they trust you and will likely value your opinion. In addition, you as the coach understand some of your players' skill sets better than they even might at their age, and helping them steer their ship relative to those skill sets is critical.

Many professional athletes also long for advice, discussions and preparation opportunities for "what's next." Professional athletes are often very bright individuals. Yes, there are some knuckleheads, but there are a lot of very bright ones, too. Many of these guys would benefit massively from opportunities to discover and prepare for a next phase of their lives. While some leagues have programs to help with this, it is something you as a coach could manage fairly easily by simply talking with your players and seeing what their future plans might entail. You could take it a step further by setting up some sort of program that helps them prepare for this, but that takes resources and time; however, it is important. This shows that you care about the player and what is next for his or her family.

Manage players not selected to All Conference, All American, National Teams, etc.: It happens to everyone at some point — even the best national team players are sometimes left off of these rosters for many reasons, some of them even personal. When those players are on your team, and they don't make a certain all-star roster or team, you could ignore it or you could manage it. Manage it.

Take time to manage those players. Take the time to chat with that player (formally or informally) about the exclusion. Every athlete is different, some will want to talk about it and make sense of it while some will want to just forget it and get after making it next time. It'll be up to you and your communication and listening skills (talked about in the next section) to determine and follow up with the athlete as needed. Put some time into this; let the athlete decide how far the conversation goes, as ignoring it could send the wrong signal to the athlete that you don't care or it's no big deal to you. Also, perhaps not making this all-star team could be a good thing. You could use this as an opportunity to have the athlete challenge himself or herself to get better so that next time he or she makes that team.

Manage nutrition: Wow, this is a big one that I don't think a lot of players, or coaches, manage properly. Players absolutely must eat well in order to perform well. The problem is that many high-level athletes do not know how or when to eat or drink appropriate things. Ensuring these high-level athletes know how to select, purchase and prepare appropriate foods is very important. In addition, discussing what they should (and shouldn't) drink and when is also key. Do not make an assumption that they know this information — this is a management issue and I would highly advise that you involve yourself.

Overall, simply take time to talk with the athlete: All of the items I mention above take communication, which is discussed in our next section. This communication is frequently done in one-on-one verbal conversations with the athlete. Take time to do this. Chat with the athlete, in the office, in the hallway, out on field, and in various places where you are finding out who they are and what is going on in their lives. Ask about their families, ask about their aspirations as people, ask about stuff related to the sport and other things as well. Manage them like a person, because that's what they are.

Youth Athlete – On Field

Managing the youth athlete and situations they will face is very different than managing adults. Kids face different challenges, from a lack of focus to changing hormones, and from growth and development issues to "unique" parental involvement issues, there are plenty of opportunities to manage. Being a proactive manager with children in youth sports is very important. If you don't stay on top of issues, both on and off the field, they can easily lead to negative outcomes.

I have a great deal of experience in managing the youth athlete and their situations. I've coached youth sports for many years, been educated in various things related to kids and sport and most importantly, I am a parent of kids in sports. Not that I've gotten every situation or conversation right, in fact some of my advice comes from massive %^@$%^-ups, but I really worked hard to manage as many facets of the youth sport experience as I could.

Take a look at the following bits of advice on how and when to manage youth athletes. I am going to start with managing practice, as I think it is a really important thing to be able to manage if you want youth athletes to be successful.

Practice: Youth athletes, depending on their age, take a massive amount of managing during their actual practices. Managing kids in a practice is exactly as it sounds: managing kids, who they are, what they do, people around them, in their sport experience. Managing kids in practices is everything from greeting them as they arrive to ensuring learning is occurring during the session.

Check out some specific ideas below. Some of the ideas in this area will bleed over/get repeated in the communication and even content sections, but they are absolutely management related.

- *Greet players by name as they arrive:* Take the time to connect with every player upon their arrival. It does not matter the age or gender of the child, they like to be greeted as they arrive. Being greeted ensures they understand you care that they are there. If they know that, they will work hard for you and the cause.

  Take it a step further by ensuring you ask them a personal question about them, their weekend, their dog, etc. The topic doesn't matter , make sure the question connects you and the child.

  Also, use their names. Not buddy or fella, or whatever else anybody else could be. Kids like to hear their name, it shows them that they know that you know who they are and it makes your comments personal.

- *Don't punish kids for being late:* Kids don't drive, their parents do. Punishing a kid for something their parent did is ridiculous. Invite them in and tell them how great it is to have them there. Think about it, if you punish the kid for being late he or she may be ashamed and then your session with him may be lost. Do you want to win an argument/battle or solve the problem/win the war? Be thoughtful about the goal here and check your emotions about promptness at the door.

  If the lateness is habitual, you have other options apart from punishment and shaming. Speak with the parents about the lateness and work with the parents on a solution. If it is an older child, perhaps you can work with him or her on ways they can assist in the process of promptness. Don't get me wrong, I still think being on time is massively critical but work toward a solution. In other words, manage.

- *Manage the first five minutes of your practice:* You don't get a second chance to make a first impression, and practice is no different, as the first five minutes is setting the tone for the day. When kids arrive, as I said above, greet them. When you start the session use "when" before "what." That is to say, before you tell them what they are going to do or with whom they will be doing, it tell them when they may do it by saying "when I say go..." This ensures that they will listen to all that is said before turning their attention to actually doing it. Don't believe me? Try it both ways and compare the results.

Get them going with short spurts of exercises to ensure their focus. With little ones, the activities are things like tag or short jogs or some other locomotor movement. This ensures they are dialed in and listening to you. For older ones it could be a longer warm-up or ball exercises. These, again, ensure they are listening and dialed in for the day. Whatever you do here make sure it is your, or the captain's, voice that they hear and that it is "managing" their attention so that they get engaged for the day.

The goal of all of this is that they are physically and mentally ready for the day. Players cannot learn if they are not focused. Get them to "dial in" to the session by getting their attention with the way you are using your voice or body language.

- *Players need to work to get it right:* This doesn't change just because the players are young. Yes, working to get it right is different with kids. Your goal should be to provide these young athletes with that environment that's focused on process over product, but you can still get them to work to improve. It is always okay to set up expectations, relative to your kids' skills and abilities, in order for them to improve and get better. Manage their effort by asking them to work as hard as they can in your sessions.

• *Players should be listening and not misbehaving:* All players should be engaged in your sessions; if they are not, don't look the other way, manage it. If players are misbehaving or not engaged take these easy steps: 1) pause, look around and say that's not good enough (punish the act not actor), 2) move on and 3) when done right say excellent, that's the way it's done.

Try not to have a go at the athlete in front of the group. Yes, they may stop what they are doing but you may lose them for that day as well. If you feel like it is a must to single out an individual make sure that it is about what they are doing (the act) vs an attack on the person (the actor). This is a critical difference and will ensure that the listening and behaving improves vs that the athlete is shamed.

Overall there are a number of different things to manage with young players during sessions. I allude to a few of them here and will do so again in greater detail in the content area. Overall, remember players, their focus, effort and attitude, must be managed in order for learning to occur. Make sure as a coach you are proactive in this process instead of just hoping or waiting for it to happen.

Ensure players know their roles and responsibilities: This is also important for young players as well as for older players. For younger players they should learn, over time, what their responsibilities are on the court or field. Usually if you can give two or three specific things that they are responsible for doing, then they have something at which to strive as well as something touchable and tangible for you to provide feedback.

Include everyone: Every player on the team should be included in the process. While some players may get more playing time it is still important that all players have some role in the team. Find a redeeming quality, or positive characteristic (perhaps it has nothing to do with actual play), accentuate that and ensure that you use it (and that they know you are using it) someway, somehow in the team.

Game day: Game day for kids is obviously different than it is for adults. Kids sometimes arrive tired or not quite ready, as they have traveled a long distance or it's early, etc. Whatever it is that may be impacting the youth athlete, here are a few things to consider as you manage him or her on game day:

- *Have them get their gear ready the night before:* Having kids pack as much of their bag the day before means that it is one less thing to do on game day.

- *Touch base with them as they arrive:* Similar to a practice, this tells them that you care that they are there and you are interested in them.

- *Ensure a warm-up that gets them mentally ready:* Kids' physiological readiness is important, but so is their mental readiness. Because kids are frequently easily distracted, the newness/excitement of game day sometimes gets the better of them. Be sure that you create a warm-up that challenges them to think, as that's what they will be asked to do in games.

- *Be sure they have eaten well:* Yes, this is off-the-field stuff but it I will include it in game day; kids need to eat well in order to perform. I would suggest, depending on the age and sport, that you do some digging around on the Internet for good pre-day, pregame and postgame meals for the youth athlete. This is a really important aspect to managing kids and it's one that doesn't get looked at enough, both for the present, and for a good foundation for the future.

- *Ensure that you have addressed the group about what you want out of the game:* Yes game day is for playing but if you are working with high-level youth athletes, and they have been training on certain things during the week, they should know that that is what you expect to see them try on game day. Communicating this is very important, as it leaves things less ambiguous and, as I mentioned earlier, it lays the foundation from which to give feedback (discussed in next section).

Review all of the items from the section for adults: All of the items from the section written for adults are also germane here. From managing bench players to managing motivation and confidence, each apply here. Athletes at different ages should be communicated with differently, but we will touch on these items in the communication section.

Youth Athlete – Off Field

When someone first starts coaching young players there is a sense that the job starts and ends with practices and games. The young coach quickly realizes that coaching is so much more than Xs and Os. In today's world of youth sports there is a lot to do to manage a team, and managing youth athletes is a multifaceted job. From managing ever-fluctuating emotions, to scheduling scrimmages, and from making sure you ensure team cohesiveness, to managing parents there is a lot to do as a youth coach.

Some youth teams are more work than others. Even at the youngest, and less competitive, ages there is much to do; especially if you are a first-time coach or volunteer coach. But as kids get older and the level is that much more competitive (high school, high-level club, etc.) there is a lot to manage — especially if you want to create and ensure that great environment.

Take a peek at the items below. You will see that some are extensions, or slightly different interpretations of, the adult pieces. You will also see a whole host of different items. Remember, as you read these, the idea is to manage the person that is the athlete and all of the things that can affect his or her development:

Make sure you have good help: I cannot stress this enough, if you are going to work with high-level young athletes, you will need assistance and that assistance will need to be managed. In many youth sports, if you are the coach there is also a manager. This person needs to be highly organized as they will help plan and coordinate travel, meals, practice games, tournaments, communication with leagues and your own school/club, etc. You should also ensure you take care of this person as they will oftentimes be putting many hours into this job for no pay. Take the time to thank them often and treat them to things now and then. Overall just be sure that they know how appreciative you are of them and how thankful you are for all that they do on a daily basis.

Manage the workload – mentally and physically: Putting kids in a competitive environment at an early age isn't inherently bad but overworking kids in that environment is bad. Some high-level sports for kids are a year-round endeavor. Again, playing and training year-round is not inherently bad as long as their play days and competitions are managed.

Be sure that kids who play year-round have time to do other things and step away from the game. Kids should have the opportunity to work different muscle groups to avoid overuse injuries as they develop. This is critical as they continue to get older and eventually specialize.

In addition, kids need down time. Providing young athletes with an opportunity to step completely away from the sport is very important. Think about it, do you like vacations? So do kids. Letting kids step away from the game that they love for a few weeks is important for their mental health and it provides them an opportunity to rediscover that passion and love for the sport (this is part of managing their motivation and confidence discussed in the environment section).

Manage parents: Okay, here we go, this one could take a while. Fortunately I have written a book on this as well called _Potentialing_. Check it out, it's a nice, short read but informative. Since I've written about the subject, I will not cover all items related to parental involvement in kid's sports. However, the truth is that you must manage parents in the youth sport setting, no matter what the age of the child, as they will have a major impact at the end of the day on how a player is managed. If you can provide helpful information on important things that will help them help their child, then your job in managing the athlete on the field just got easier.

I am going to include a few things below but the key is to basically communicate effectively and in a timely manner with each family. Remember they think their child > team > club/school whereas you think club/school > team > child. What I meaning by this is that your starting place is different than their starting place. Even before you begin a conversation, remember they always want what is best for their child whereas you often start from a place that, yes, has their child's development in mind, but that also has the best interests of the school and team in mind, too.

- *Help parents manage car rides with their kids:* Sometimes parents want to solve all of the world's problems, or at least ones their son or daughter is facing in sport, during this car ride to or from practices and games. Tell them, gently, that this is bad and actually counterproductive. Help parents understand that this is a time for young athletes to decompress or ready themselves for a game. Asking them what they want to eat or how do they feel is great. Giving them instructions for, or deconstructing their performance that day is not great. Ensure parents understand that this car ride is a chance for them to be a helpful parent, not an instructive coach.

- *Help them with nutrition advice:* What and when kids eat needs to be managed. Unfortunately, you don't control that, parents do. Provide parents with logical nutrition and hydration advice that you can easily find online or by consulting a nutritionist. Taking the time to manage this aspect with parents will go a long way to helping your kids perform better on the field or court.

- *Touch base often*: Taking time to chat with parents frequently can nip problems in the bud. Parents want information, and frequently, about their child. This information can be anything from how their child is doing or feeling to what tournaments or games are coming up and when. Stay on top of this communication as problems occur when people don't know things. Make the communication formal (emails or one-on-one meetings, for example) and informal (chats at the gym or field, a text message or two, etc.). You will find that the more you (or our manager) touches base, the better it is when something of concern comes up, as it will likely be a legitimate concern vs something trivial.

- *Game days:* Give parents some ideas on how to prepare for and handle themselves on game days. Preparation for game day can be ideas for parents on things like when or what to eat, that they should pack the bag the day before game, that they should lay the uniform out for the morning, and so on. These should be ideas that make the time before the game less chaotic and more predictable; this provides control for the young athlete and leads to great calmness and less anxiety.

Parents should understand what their role during the game is. They should understand that you are the coach and their role is to support the team and their child.

- *Give them tips on how they can handle their child's ups and downs*: Kids will experience multiple successes and failures as young athletes. Educating parents that these things happen often, this is what they mean and this is how to handle them in order to ensure that their kids enjoy their experience, stay motivated and confident and continue to develop. For a list of ideas on how parents can handle successes and failures with an eye to keeping their kids excited and motivated, check out my book or research things like "managing kids' success" or "managing kids' failures" in sport.

- *Get to know the parents as people:* As you continue to manage the youth athlete and their parents, remember parents are people, too. Take time to find out about them as people by asking them questions about what they enjoy or like to do away from their children or the sport. You may actually find that many of these people are quite engaging and, as a result, you will likely manage them and their children differently because of this finding.

You are the head of your particular company, be it a youth sports team, college team or pro team. How you manage this company will have a great deal to do with how well you do your job and, ultimately, how well your group performs on the court or field. In addition, how you manage people will basically ensure whether or not you are instilling a great environment and building your presence in order for you to do your job effectively.

Take the time to consider all of the things that you need to do to manage the minutia in your particular position. Write these things down and set a plan for how, and with whom, you will go about managing these items. Put this plan to work and watch your environment get built. Of course nobody can manage if they can't communicate effectively, but fortunately for you, that's next.

Chapter 6

Communication

In order to have presence, manage people and create an environment that ensures performance there must be communication. This truly is what it all comes down to because if you can't communicate your thoughts and ideas, there is no way you can have successful teams, let alone a successful coaching career. And, most importantly, there is no way to establish the all-important relationship that it takes to work with people in sport.

We communicate our thoughts and feelings to our athletes (and others) all of the time whether we intend to or not. Moreover, what we communicate massively impacts, positively or negatively, the people we are coaching. But do we know what we are doing? Are we methodical? More importantly, can we be thought-filled enough to ensure we are using our communication skills to ensure we are building our presence, managing our athletes and creating an environment of excellence over time and in ever-changing, pressure-filled situations so that our athletes thrive?

When you think about communicating with others in a pressure situation, think about how and when you like to be communicated with. When you are trying something new, do you like someone hovering over you picking apart your every move? What about when you are doing something that you worked really hard on that you are performing or doing for the first time in front someone, for a grade or a raise or a promotion? Or when you have put a lot of time into something, come up short and know you have erred; do you like it when someone cares enough to chat you up about it? Or when you are having some life troubles there is someone there for you to chat with? Yes, we are all different, but many of those items above have very similar answers, especially if the communication is coming from someone who you trust and who is impacting your development/job/future.

Communication seems simple enough. According to Webster's Dictionary communication is "the act or process of using words, sounds, signs, or behaviors to express or exchange information or to express your ideas, thoughts, feelings, etc., to someone else." It is essentially made up of verbal, nonverbal and listening skills — that's it. Verbal means spoken words; nonverbal means gestures and use of the body to communicate thoughts and feelings; while listening is the receiving of information from someone else. How hard is that? Of course, what separates great communicators from poor communicators is how and when they employ these skills. And, more importantly for us, is how a great coach would use these communication skills to ensure he or she built presence, managed situations and people, and built a great environment.

The label of a great communicator is often bestowed upon a coach not just by the outside world, but by his or her players. Let's take Pete Carroll, coach of the 2014 NFL Super Bowl-winning Seattle Seahawks. For starters, Coach Carroll is a very successful coach, having won championships at both the college and professional levels. But more than championship winning teams Coach Carroll is known for being a great communicator, a positive coach who manages his players as people and ensures there is a positive and encouraging environment that strives for greatness.

So what is it about Coach Carroll that makes him special? Firstly, Coach Carroll is said to have a list of eight items that he uses as his mantra. Among items in this list are ensure your athletes always compete, motivate your athletes, create a great environment and nurture your players as people. But of course also on this list, and something that coach Carroll is known for, is be a great communicator.

Coach Carroll appears to be a positive coach who gets in the ear of all of his players and ensures his players know what is expected and where they stand with him. Coach Carroll is said to be a players' coach because he coaches them up by being positive and encouraging in a league that isn't used to that. Make no mistake, Coach Carroll is probably quite demanding, but by all accounts he pulls players aside and talks with them, not at them (listening as well as talking), finds out about them as people and ensures that the effort that they are putting in is nothing less than 100 percent, and for the good of the team.

It's not just the players that Coach Carroll is said to communicate well with; it is "others" as well. Coach Carroll is masterful with the media, fielding questions with calmness, candor, humor or whatever the mood seems to call for and seemingly having a knack for how and when to say what in order to come off as a genuine person. He is also said to be caring and thoughtful with his staff, ensuring that they have the freedom to make choices within their jobs (offensive, defensive, special teams, etc.) and communicating with them changes that need to be made, things they are doing well or poorly as well as personal topics about them as people.

Coach Carroll has built an environment of excellence by appearing to manage his athletes and staff through his positivity and fantastic communication abilities. Deconstructing coaches like Pete Carroll can give us a lot of insight into what exactly great communicators do on a daily basis. More importantly for us, and for the purposes of this section of this book, we should see how a great coach uses his or her communication to manage their athletes and families, to build their great environment and, of course, as it lends itself to building the presence of that coach.

In the previous chapters I have actually mentioned a number of key communication items that coaches do in order to build presence, create an environment and manage situations and people; without actually saying they were "communication" items. For a refresher on details of those items flip back to those sections. Below is a quick reminder of some of the communication items from other sections.

Presence: Using your voice and the tone in your voice to ensure certain things get done (maintain focus and calm, for example), talking with the athlete vs at the athlete, using body language wisely.

Environment: Stress the process over the product (redefine success), coach the person not the athlete, build trust, build their motivation from within, build their bank of success, establish that mind-set of expectations and foundations for player success, ask them to problem solve vs tell them what to do.

Management: Most items in this section are examples of when and how a good coach communicates. I would suggest you read the items below and then reread the management section with the items in mind, they make the items in this section pop just a bit more.

These items are key, but they are just some of the things that communicative coaches do to be great. In the remainder of the section you will see that I lay out some items I have seen good coaches do in terms of communicating with their athletes as well as with those that surround the athlete. Not that these items are earth-shatteringly new, but they are massive in terms of how they relate to the presence, management and environment that a good coach creates. Moreover, I would argue that if you look at any good coach out there they do these things well.

You will also see that I have not separated anything by age or gender. This is because I believe a good communicator is a good communicator, regardless of the age or gender to which they are communicating. Clearly if one is coaching a younger athlete the communication would be massively different in terms of what would need to be done to ensure proper learning and development, but I will cover some of that minutia that would be age-specific once I get into the content section. Coaches who are good communicators do all of the following things well.

Give Constructive Criticism

Good coaches ensure that their words and actions act as behavior change agents as opposed to destroyers. Meaning, the words that these coaches use are meant to ensure that the athlete gets better as a result of the communication. This can be on the field of play as a player tries something and needs feedback to improve, or off the field where perhaps they make a choice that needs some feedback that helps correct the behavior. The feedback that is given will help the athlete change his or her behavior for the better, try it this way, what about doing it like this, that's okay but how about this, all examples of ensuring expectations and giving constructive criticism in order that the athlete can improve.

Punish the Act, Not the Actor

Listen, sometimes coaches have to have a go at something that is going on that isn't good enough — as they should. As I said earlier. athletes of all ages need to be managed and that management sometimes comes in the form of "that is not acceptable" or "that is not good enough." But the good coach will ensure that those statements are made toward the behavior that is unacceptable as opposed to being directed at the person. "You aren't good enough" vs "that is not good enough" are two vastly different phrases. Good coaches take the time to ensure that they are having a go at the act as opposed to the actor.

Give Clear, Detailed Information

You will notice that coaches who communicate understand how to spot things and then give feedback to the athlete about that thing such that the athlete understands. They notice something that the athlete did well or poorly and can spot that behavior or choice. Once spotted, they can provide detailed information about that choice, be it on the field or off the field, and ensure that the athlete understands what it is. This necessitates a couple of things: 1) that the coach knows what he or she expects and wants (this is a content issue and will be discussed in detail later and 2) the coach understands the level of the athlete and has the right words to convey these thoughts to the athlete such that the athlete sees that detail and can rectify the situation and/or make sense of the compliment.

Are Timely With Words

Timing just might be everything for an athlete. When athletes are performing in training they need words that encourage or adjust their behavior in order that the skill is learned and performed correctly. A good coach delivers this information not only clearly and with detail (see above), but also at the right time so that the athlete can make adjustments/accept a compliment and connect it with the behavior. Another example is when an athlete has had something happen off of the field. A good communicator can spot this, as perhaps he is listening to the signs, and engages the athlete in a timely manner to ensure they are okay. Coaches don't always get this right but the goods ones strive to ensure they are timely with their feedback and constructive criticisms.

Have Body Language Awareness

Again, I know I said this earlier but it bears repeating, good coaches are very aware of their body language and what it is saying. All you have to do is go to my example person from the beginning of this section — Pete Carroll — and go find a clip of him: it really looks like he knows he is being watched. His body language is most often very positive and that positivity matches his philosophy and what he wants out of his environment, and that is contagious, especially when you are winning!

Body language doesn't always have to be positive but as a coach you must always be aware that you are being watched and your body language will make an impact. If you want to make a point in your environment, or while you are managing, do so, but be aware of how powerful those pictures are to the recipient. Be ready to follow up with words as you see others seeing you as it may require a follow-up conversation. Bottom line is that good coaches are very aware of their body language and use it to make a point, to players, media and others!

Defend Their Players

I love to watch this one in action. There is nothing that wins a player over more than defending that player in front of media, other players, parents or fans. I've seen this at every level. Perhaps a player has had a few bad games or events and is being criticized by whomever. The easiest thing for a coach to do would be to come and pile on; not sure how that helps. Instead of jumping on the obvious, the coach defends the player to anyone who will listen. Citing certain reasons that may be real or not real, they defend that player to others, and so that the player can hear as well.

The coach does this for many reasons. One, being that perhaps it is the truth. Another reason might be that the coach knows he needs the player, and perhaps the player is really close to turning it around but just needs that little bit of positivity to others. Yes, there may be times that the coach can't do this but the good ones know how and when to use this to ensure the player is defended and hears that defense.

Keep Negative Comments "In House"
Instead of Airing Dirty Laundry

Bashing your player or bad situations that happen within your team to other people is no bueno. Good, experienced, coaches understand that negative things, whether with an individual player or within your team or organization, happen. The good communicator ensures that these items are dealt with and dealt with swiftly but they are handled in house and not gossiped about or dealt with out and about.

Yes, it sometimes feels really good to air grievances to others, but be careful. The unintended consequences of talking about things that are happening within your team are too many to count. In addition, trying to rectify those situations or problems becomes harder when that stuff is in the open. Good coaches take the time to handle these issues face to face and ensure that they stay in that small circle in order to find a solution.

Use Honest Words

If you want to build trust amongst your athletes and within your team, you must be honest with your players. Sometimes the truth stings, and you have to be smart about when and how you communicate honestly with your athletes. But being honest with players is critical for building a foundation of trust and being able to manage effectively.

Things like why a player was on the bench, or why the player has changed positions, or why the player hasn't made the roster are all things that players prefer to hear about in an honest way from you in person. Delivering this information needs to be done in a timely fashion, not right before game time and you need to be prepared to have a follow-up question about why and what they can do to improve. But it is much better to hear it from you than to read it somewhere or hear it from someone else or in an email. Good coaches take the time to be honest and up front with their players in order to build trust.

Connect With Players (Empathy)

The best communicators have an ability to connect with their athletes because they truly care for them and how they feel/are doing. As you see good coaches speak with their players you can see that there is an empathy for who the person is and what he or she is going through. This is at the heart of my statements, you coach a person you don't coach an athlete; and, talk with the person not at the person. Good coaches take the time to know what their athletes may be experiencing. Knowing this, the coach works to connect a that player based on the player's context (their background, where they are from, etc.) not his or her (the coach's) context. Taking this extra step can go a long way to ensuring a meaningful, impactful conversation.

Engage Athletes With Energy and Passion

As you watch that good coach, you will see that he or she always show ups. By that I mean the good communicator can ensure that no matter what is going on with them that day they bring the requisite energy for that practice/game/team talk. Sometimes the situation calls for something with spice and sometimes it calls for time, but no matter what the occasion athletes can see that the coach cares deeply about what they are doing.

Good coaches know that there is a time for a loud voice and a time for a soft voice but they always ensure that their passion and energy shine through. This takes good use of tone, timing and choice of words, all things learned in time.

Treat Each Person As An Individual

Everybody is different and so is every athlete. As a result each athlete needs to be communicated with differently. Some need to be talked with often while others do not, some need to be asked more things than told, and others respond better to loud while others to soft. Whatever the case, athletes are all different and as a result in order to get the most out of them they each need to be communicated with differently.

Treat Athletes Fairly, Not Equally

Good coaches know that all athletes need to be held to a certain standard but that each athlete is not created equally. This is an extension of the suggestion above that each person should be worked with differently as they are all unique. The idea here is that, for example, a veteran player should not only be spoken with differently because he or she has earned it, and while this may not appear as being equal to others in the mix, it is certainly fair. Veteran players, for example, have a different understanding of the game and, as a result, should be spoken with and worked with differently. The standard expectations are still there and evident but how you get there with that type of player vs a rookie is different.

Be sure athletes understand why, for example, someone is being treated differently. If left to their own devices players will come to their own conclusions about why someone is being treated differently. It has been my experience that once everyone understands that everyone is being treated fairly but differently all is good.

Use Humor Wisely
(Not Sarcasm Toward the Individual)

This is 100 percent part of being a good communicator. Remember, you are a person and so are players and, as a result, there are times where a bit of banter and or high-brow humor is key. Some of you reading this may be functioning in a highly competitive and pressure-filled sporting environment, and to be able to drop a funny line or two at the right time can really help you manage your athletes and ensure that the environment is one where people want to be day in and day out.

This is not to say be sarcastic or have fun at someone else's expense. Your humor should not negatively impact someone else. First off, sarcasm is never good, since it is often misunderstood and not inclusive. Also, having fun at someone else's expense isn't fun, as long as it's not you. Be inclusive with your humor and use it wisely but for goodness sake, have some banter.

Read the Audience (See Presence For More)

This is a follow-up point from the presence section, but it is important to read the mood of your group and communicate accordingly. As I have said a few times already, sometimes a group needs a kick in the ass, and sometimes they need humor, and sometimes they need a calm talk. How can you know unless you take the time to gauge where they are and what they need?

Some refer to this as "taking the pulse of your group" and this is probably the perfect picture to paint as if a group is too hot, and you give them a hot drink it is not good for business. Gauging your group takes time and a real awareness. Take time to really see what your group is feeling (empathy) and then manage them from there.

Optimistic vs Pessimistic Explanatory Style

Do you like to be around people who see the glass half full or half empty? Coaches who are good communicators inspire hope and a "we can do this" type of approach as opposed to one who sees gloom and doom because of a few bad outings and experiences.

This needs to get communicated to others via words and, more importantly, actions. Words from a coach to the effect of "we can do this" and "keep going" are powerful, but body language and actions are even more powerful. If athletes hear you saying positive things but then see you freaking out or displaying body language that would suggest that the end is near, it will negatively impact your environment and they may follow suit!

The great communicator stays focused on what the group can do vs what the group can't do. This will really get tested when things aren't going well. This is truly when good coaches are made, as it's easy to be optimistic when things are going well, but what about when all seems lost, how will you be?

Are Front and Center When Things Are Good and Bad

This is for sure a case where a picture is worth a thousand words. It's easy to be out there and talking when you have won, but where will you be when you have lost? Great coaches take the bad with the good and are there to lean on during both times. The great ones ensure that their groups don't get too high or too low in wins or losses. But no matter what, the great coach shows body language of "I am here no matter what in order to manage you and this environment."

Listen

I've deliberately left this one until the end because I think it is critical to each of the suggestions above. Communication is a two-way street. Great coaches understand that they must, yes, talk and ensure their message is heard, but also listen to their players; both in what they are saying and what they are not saying.

Some coaches listen just enough in order that they may ascertain the meaning and then they crowbar their two cents in as soon as possible. Great coaches take time to truly hear what the players have to say and then determine how they may be able to help as a result of that listening. Or perhaps they are just listening to listen to listen and that's okay, too. I am not suggesting that the great coach has to listen all the time, as sometimes it is not the time to listen, but like anything the great coach understands timing and when is the right time to talk vs listen.

With all of these suggestions in the communication section it should be apparent that, above all else, the great coach is a person who works hard at working with his or her athletes in order to accomplish what is best for the team. The coaches who are exceptional communicators have an ability to connect with their players, talk with them vs at them, listen well and have exceptional timing for how and when they communicate. Moreover, I would argue that anyone can be good at communicating as long as he or she starts with the best interest of the athlete in mind and puts himself or herself out there to work at this vital skill in many different situations. Above all else, remember, you are coaching people not athletes.

Summary of the 4 Elements

The elements of Presence, Environment, Management and Communication are the 4 critical elements that make up a great coach. When I work with groups and lay these elements out, I always challenge people to do some deconstructing on their own. Use the elements as context and watch great coaches — on TV, in print, in person — then do what they do. It is always more powerful when you take somebody you admire and pick apart how they work with their teams. Then, for those who aspire to be great coaches of people, I suggest taking what we talked about relative to these elements and going out and practicing this stuff.

Getting great at each of these elements takes focused effort and time. As you will see in the following two sections, Content and Experience, there are a number of concrete things in addition to these elements that a coach must do to be great. But, the great ones use these 4 elements to drive at how they teach their sport, as well as how they gain experiences in order to be great.

Section 3 – *Content and Teaching Content*

Let's just say for argument's sake that you are a math teacher, new to teaching, but you have presence and an ability to create a great environment by managing your students through very effective communication. However, you don't really understand math all that well or have an ability to teach someone how to do math. You will likely have a great environment with effectively managed students who will know nothing about math!

Now let's flip that around and talk about a math teacher, new to teaching and who has an ability in, and an understanding of how to teach, math. He or she has a sense of the content and likely even has a few math exercises and perhaps even a curriculum that he or she is looking to ensure gets taught. This person, although new, has a very important ingredient in coaching — he or she has content and a bit of an understanding of how to teach that content.

Bottom line — you need to know your subject backward and forward and how you want teach someone that subject in order to be great at what you do. You can have all 4 elements and still be a terrible soccer coach because you are a basketball coach. Meaning, just because you have the 4 elements doesn't automatically make you a great coach, but in order to be a great coach you will need the 4 elements.

As a coach in sport, you must know the content that you are going to teach your athletes and you must know how to teach the content. More importantly, and germane to this book, it is important that you know and teach this content with the person at the forefront of your mind. When I say content I am referring to the technical, tactical, physical and psychological aspects that are critical to the level of the person and sport that one is coaching. Most people who begin to coach their sport know their sport a bit and have a sense of what they might want to teach their players. But many of them, like perhaps a well-equipped new math teacher, lack ideas on the content and how to present that content to learners in order to maximize the learning experience for people.

If you look at any of the people I have chosen to use as examples thus far they all know their content backward and forward and are masterful at presenting (teaching) their content to people who are athletes. Think about John Wooden, Jose Mourinho, Pat Summitt, and so on, yes, they are masters at the 4 elements, which helps them as teachers, but a more important yes is that they are master teachers. Let's face it — that is what we are talking about here — these people are master teachers who use the 4 elements and their understanding of their sport to teach people their sport.

So what is it that these coaches do? You will see that in the next section in which I outline what "content" and "curriculum" can mean to a person who is putting the person and the relationship first. Then I outline specific things that great coaches, master teachers, do on a daily basis to ensure that they are coaching the person first as they coach people in their sport. If you are pursuing coaching as a career you should be attending coaching education programs for your sport. The items included here will provide you with some initial ideas on developing or selecting content as well as ideas. Formal coach education programs will provide a great deal more on the specific content and teaching methodologies relative to your sport.

As you read the specific examples in the "teaching content" section you will notice that there are a lot of items that come directly from the 4 elements section — perfect. What I am trying to do here is use those as a guide to show some specific examples of those elements and how one might use those with their people daily in practice. Read each of the next two chapters with a person-first perspective and with all of the 4 elements in mind.

Chapter 7

Content

Over the years I have observed master coaches use their relationship to coach the people who are in their respective programs. These master coaches had a presence, created a great environment, managed their athletes and had fantastic communication. But more than anything they knew their game very well and were sensational teachers. They had a system of play that they believed in and a way to teach that system to their players. They all had a bevy of exercises and ideas that taught the game in unique ways and had a knack for ensuring that the skills and abilities within those exercises were taught and ultimately learned.

Think John Wooden, Phil Jackson, Jose Mourinho. These coaches appear to have all 4 elements in spades, but more than anything they are known for how their teams played. Technically proficient, organized and disciplined defense, but of course how they "play" is a result of what they did in trainings and games. It was in these trainings where these coaches ensured that their content or *curriculum* was taught and learned.

What is curriculum? A loaded question for sure but basically it is any or all subjects or tasks in a course of study — your content. In school, for example, it is all of the courses (math, science, humanities) that make up one's degree along with the skills/concepts within each of those courses (addition and subtraction, in math). A good teacher has a multitude of lessons and activities that he or she uses to teach these subjects and skills. That's the easy part for the teacher. The good teacher then takes those lessons and makes them magic by teaching the contents of the curriculum in a way that learners learn.

Of course in sports, then, curriculum includes the skills, tactics and systems that make up the sport (passing, dribbling, zonal defending, etc.) and then the skills within each of those skills and abilities (how to pass, how to receive, etc., in passing). A good coach has a multitude of drills and exercises that he or she uses as a platform to teach these skills and tactics. Again, this is the easy part as these games, drills and exercises are readily available online, in books or learned in coaching education programs. It's not to say that you would know how and when to use these exercises, but they are available. The good coach is the one who can take this curriculum — this content — and make it magic by teaching the skills embedded within the exercises.

This is huge. The great coach and novice coach can run the same activity yet the good coach makes the exercise pop for the people involved while the novice coach is just running the drill. This is partly due to the items outlined in the 4 elements sections, plus experience, and what we will address below regarding one's ability. In the meantime, let's define how one knows what to teach.

How do you know what to teach? This is a common question with emerging coaches, as, how can you know? Some novices step into a coaching situation where there is a prescribed curriculum. If this is the case then do what is asked. Whereas others need to come up with a direction on their own. Perhaps we can start with the question of what would the great ones do or WWGD?

Many of the great ones start from the game and work backward. Meaning, they look at the game and pick it apart to see what they should be teaching to their athletes. It is certainly a starting place, but there is of course so much more that great coaches do to ensure they are teaching what they need to be teaching.

I have created and implemented sport curriculum locally, nationally and internationally for youth clubs, professional clubs, organizations and school districts. While all sports and levels are different many of the principles for creating and implementing content are the same. And, relative to this book, they are similar to the way great coaches around the world at various levels in different sports create and implement their curriculum with and for people not just athletes.

Before we dive into these ideas for creating curriculum/content, let me paint a picture of curriculum by giving an analogy. When explaining curriculum with the person or relationship first I often use the idea of a map. A map is something we are all familiar with as it gives you a sense of the "area" or "place" at which you are looking. More importantly, a map is something that many people use to see where they may be going together, perhaps on a trip together. If we were going on a trip using our map as a guide we would need to use it to determine a couple of things. First we would need to determine where we want to go, and we also would need to know our starting place. And, of course, we would need to use the map to determine the best way to get from our starting point to our destination.

The best curricula for content in the world — used by coaches or schools — is constructed like a map. The curriculum would have a detailed picture of where you will end, where you will start and how you will get there — as a collaborative group. People who design this curriculum know their terrain backward and forward and as a result provide massive amounts of detail in this curriculum map. And, of course, these experts are also expert guides, using the 4 elements, and their excellent teaching skill, to guide their people through this curriculum to ensure they successfully arrive at their intended destination.

The items below are things that great coaches do to ensure they are coaching what needs to be coached for the people involved in their sport. I use the map analogy to paint a picture of how and why these things are being done. Take these ideas as starters for what all good curricula should have as a base, and build from there.

1. Have a Philosophy (The Foundation of Your Map)

The philosophy will serve as the foundation on which you will build your map. It will determine the font, scale, colors, topography, and details that make up your map. The beginning, middle and end will make up the details in the map but this is your guide to creating the basic structure of your map.

You must have a philosophy about who you are as a person and what you expect as a coach. Abstractly, a coaching philosophy is a set of ideas and principles that guide you as a person and coach. These principles should help you determine what, why and how you will be doing as you coach. In addition, these principles will help you determine what objectives are important for you to reach and how you will reach those objectives.

Nick Saban's principles, John Wooden's Pyramid, Pete Carroll's 8 Rules are all examples of a coaching philosophy. I guarantee that every great coach has some sort of guiding principles that govern exactly what he or she expects as a coach. The really good ones start with broad principles and boil those down into very specific things. For example, being aggressive in how you play is a broad topic. For instance, these people get to their daily session with ideas on how they teach a certain topic, like defending, and will likely encompass some sort of very aggressive approach.

Write your philosophy down. Write it down so that you can see it, refine it and stay true to it. If you are new to coaching do not reinvent the wheel. Most people imitate before they innovate. Take time to understand someone else's philosophy that you agree with or look up to, and use that as a starter kit. Use those ideas, try them out, change them over time and make your own in time. No matter what, take the time to write out what you expect from yourself and others, as having a philosophy will help you make decisions for your sessions and players as you begin to coach.

Note: as we look at the destination, starting place and path for our content (curriculum) you should understand that we will need to take all three things into account as we build our content. Meaning that I will talk about starting with the destination in mind to determine where we should go with our curriculum. But of course our destination and path to get to the destination will always change once we establish our starting place. Keep this idea in mind as you read each example below. Once done with all three you will hopefully see how they fit together nicely as you think about what content and curriculum is right for you and your sport.

2. The Map...

The Destination – Know Where You Want To Get To

Again, using the map analogy, how can you know, how you will arrive at a destination if you haven't picked a destination? Pick the destination.

Where do you want your people to be by the end of your season or seasons, depending on your sport? Do you have them for a year? Okay, what do they need to know by the end of that year. This is no different than having standards that a third grader would be striving to reach by the end of the year — in spelling or math, for example. You absolutely must have an idea of where you want to be at certain times throughout that year in order for you to have any sense of what to do day in and day out. Great coaches know where they are going and they set benchmarks throughout the year to determine how close or far away they are from the goal of these benchmarks throughout the year.

As I said previously, many coaches start from the game and work backward to determine the best path to take in order to arrive at their destination. Many coaches are students of the game that they are teaching and as a result when they watch the game they don't just watch it, they deconstruct it. They constantly ask themselves things like why is that team playing like they are playing and how did they get there, why are those players are doing that and how did they learn that, how did that player do that skill and how can they learn that, etc. By asking these questions they are working backward from the game to determine what to teach.

Take time to write down the skills and concepts that you expect your players to have by the end and certain times during the year. These can be technical abilities, motor skills, tactical concepts and mental abilities. This can also be your system of play that you hope to employ.

Use these as your goals and objectives for the year. Be as detailed as possible and set measureable benchmarks to determine progress towards these end points.

It is beyond the scope of this book to determine specific end points and systems for various sports, levels and ages. But, again, there is a vast amount of information on many sports levels and ages available online, in print or in good coach education programs. Find some of these and work from there.

Most importantly though, ensure that this destination is in line with your philosophy. The skills and abilities you determine are important to your sport need to be in line with who you are and what you believe. After all, having a map on which you can't find your destination can't ever be good!

The Starting Place

Of course how can you know where you are going when you don't know where you are starting? When people start coaching they oftentimes neglect a fundamental thing: what is the starting place for their athletes? I have seen many new coaches start with an exercise that is so far above the players' heads that the players are left frustrated and, of course, have very little success. So we must consider this as we think about what we will include, and where we will begin, in our curriculum. Below are some specific things you should consider as you think about the starting place for your athletes.

**Age of the athlete:** Different ages are capable of different things. When I am working with coaches of younger groups I ask them to consider the cognitive, emotional, physical and motor starting places of the athletes. This will, of course, impact the destination (so, yes, you will have to go back and change the destination, but that's okay).

There are multiple researchers out there who can help establish some age-appropriate guidelines for your athletes. Sometimes it's as easy as researching "age appropriate sessions for 12-year-olds," as an example.

No matter what, consider the age of the athlete and what you can expect in terms of the aforementioned starting places.

Level of the athlete: In school a teacher must know the starting place of, for example, their 16-year-old math student. If you give too difficult an assignment you may lose him or her. If you give an assignment that is too easy they will be bored and not challenged. You must consider how comfortable they are in the subject before you move them along the continuum. Similarly in sport, sometimes a coach will put very difficult exercises or drills into a session and expect that the athletes can do it. The coach really needs to consider the level of the athletes prior to starting the year, month and of course, first day. Start by watching them play. See what level they are at and create some exercises that demand that level of focus, expertise and intensity. Similar to the math student, if you give them too much for too many days they will quit: give them not enough and they get bored.

In time you can push them. Understand that this is their starting place and that their level can change. Challenge them. You will see that in the section below I talk about some ways to challenge your athletes during sessions.

Know what the athlete knows: This is slightly different than the level of the player as perhaps these athletes are good athletes at a decent level but they lack certain things a higher caliber athlete needs. I have seen players who play at a very high level but who are clearly lacking in a certain area. Again, like a student who is very bright, perhaps the math skills are fantastic but the writing skills need work, okay, that needs to be worked on. Determine what skills and ideas players are lacking. These skills and concepts should be relative to your end points or standards (your destination) you set as their end points. In addition, these skills should be relative to their level of play. As you improve what the athletes know and can do you will likely be increasing their level as well. In addition, in time these will be moving you closer to your destination, but you see this is getting us into our path!

The Path – Establish Topics

Establish topics that you will do on a daily, weekly, monthly basis with your athletes, relative to you starting place, to help you reach your destination on your map. Some coaches will be comfortable looking at the entire year and saying okay, we will do these topics on these days, these weeks and these months, and can fill their calendar out early. Others will not be so comfortable so they set out their calendar for a month, or even week at a time. Still others prefer to do a hybrid of sorts; work to address certain topics for the first eight sessions, play a game, and then determine what to include after they see their athletes play.

Again, using the map as an analogy, many travelers have different ways they like to travel as they weave their way to their destination. Some know their route right away, some play it day-by-day, but they are all headed to that same end point. Whatever path you take is your call. But, whatever you do, establish a plan.

Establish a plan: Set out how you will move along your path. It's not to say that you can't change course, but having a plan for skills or concepts you will hit at a certain point along your path is important. By establishing these things you can have a target at which you are aiming. Be as detailed as you can early on by establishing skills to be hit on these days, concepts to be hit on these days and exact targets to be hit at certain months.

Feel free to change direction: Remember your goal is to coach the person and, as a result you must be able to be flexible in your journey. For example, you have an end point, and you have a starting point, and you have established your path, but you have played some games and see deficiencies. Great, sit down, assess where you are and where you aren't. This "assessment" can be anything from breaking down film to assessing players individually to simply eyeballing your group and saying a change is needed. The worst thing you can do is continue on a path that you feel in your heart of hearts is wrong — that'll get you lost!

Take breaks: Just like when you are traveling, you will need breaks. The idea of periodization in sports is critical. Periodization simply refers to cycles that players go through during their season or playing career. It is their ups and downs and highs and lows, both physically and mentally. Players need breaks as they cannot play at a highest level without coming back down a bit. The good coach can spot these times, the bad coach will continue to grind his or her athletes and push them further down the rabbit hole where some will not make it out.

I would encourage you to really do some looking around on how players of different ages in similar sports hit their peaks and valleys. Knowing this will make a big difference in how you are able to change directions midseason. The important thing is to understand that it is very difficult to drive straight through at a high rate of speed to any far destination.

Creating a curriculum map isn't easy, but it is imperative if you are going to get from point 'A' to point 'B' with (and for) somebody on purpose. Yes, you may arrive at a destination without using a map but when this happens perhaps your mode of transportation was just bigger, stronger and faster than everyone else — which is often the case in sports at many levels. The good coach takes these big, strong, fast athletes and creates a curriculum that ensures they have the opportunity to become better people as well as bigger, stronger and faster.

Hopefully you have seen how a great coach creates his or her content or curriculum. It is a daunting task for some new coaches but, as I said earlier, imitate before you innovate. There are so many good resources out there about what you might be able to teach athletes in your sport. Find these great coaches or great resources and learn as much as you can about what they teach. Immersing yourself in someone else's way of thinking will provide you a lot of insight into not only what they do, but why (their philosophy) they do it.

Content takes time to build and even more time to get right. Take your time in learning, and then creating, and eventually implementing your curriculum with your athletes. Write it out and hold yourself accountable since, over time and if your work at it, it will change and morph into something quite special. Think about the examples I have used; these people are all much older, which tells me they toiled for many years with the elements and content in order to be great. Of course what makes these people, and perhaps you, special isn't the content but how that content is taught.

Chapter 8

Teaching Content

Over the years I have seen some incredible drills and exercises in many sports that look to try to ensure content gets taught, and they dazzle the eye in the process. Players set up here, balls being fed in from there and players doing all sorts of patterns and movement in order to get to the basket or goal. Sadly, though, in many of these activities players were perhaps getting through the obstacle course of stuff but getting very little out of it. Why? Well, as I said above, a recipe is only as good as the chef and so a drill or exercise is only as good as the coach. The devil is in the details.

How you teach is as important (or more) as what you teach. Yes, you need good curricula but ensuring that your content gets taught is obviously important to how well your team plays in games and, ultimately, how quickly and successfully they reach their destination. If you have read this far hopefully you can see that the 4 elements are basically a how-to guide for teaching people. By that I mean, if you have incorporated those elements into your repertoire you are well on your way to teaching your athletes the "how-to's" of being a great person and athlete.

Think back to my examples of John Wooden, Alex Ferguson, Nick Saban and others. They ensure that they are teaching their people that happen to be athletes by having a presence, creating a great environment, managing situations and people and communicating effectively. Of course these aren't the only things they do to ensure their messages get across, but by doing these things really well they are able to ensure that they tick off a number of boxes for what makes a good teacher of information.

In the 4 elements section I have tried to describe conceptual ideas as well as detailed things these great coaches, and great coaches in general, do to ensure athletes become better off and on the field. The concepts, such as talk with vs at, build your voice, build players' banks of success are presented in order to paint that broad picture of what great coaches do and what you can do to be that great coach as well. But I have also tried to provide some detailed ideas on how and when, for instance, you can build players' banks of success. For the remainder of the content section I would like to focus our attention on these items, plus add a few more, to ensure details from your content are taught, thoughtfully, and ultimately learned in practice.

Great coaches are great teachers, period. More importantly, great coaches use training sessions as a time to teach their players life lessons as well as important things they would like to have them do in competitions and games. Basically, training sessions are a coach's time to be detailed with how they teach their content by implementing each of the 4 elements plus a few more items.

I contend that if you were to walk out to a master coach's training session you could quantitatively assess their training session by rating them in key areas of each of the 4 elements plus a few more items that I will describe below. In fact, I have done this for both master coaches as well as emerging coaches and it is fascinating. In almost any practice I have watched a master coach conduct, the master coach impresses as he or she creates an environment full of expectations as well as opportunities for players to think and build motivation and confidence. I see them manage their athletes throughout the session and communicate effectively in order that their athletes are working through their failures and improving on, at the end of the day, the content that is being taught that day.

More importantly, and relative to this book and particularly this chapter, I have watched novice coaches work through their practice sessions and do well in some areas and struggle through others. This is great, as the coach is working through his or her content and lesson plan in order to teach their people on that day. What I enjoy most is, after watching the coach run the session, we chat about what they have done well or what they have done poorly, relative to the 4 elements and additional items. This, of course, serves to move them along the coaching continuum and build the experience(s) (next section).

As I have said, coaching is more than simply running an exercise. Looking at a coach's training session, we should be able to assess how well or poorly he or she is working with people to ensure they are teaching their athletes the ideas embedded in the session, activity or drill. I also believe that you don't need someone else to assess you on these items to ensure you improve. Yes, it helps, but let's face it, assessors interested in moving you along a continuum aren't always available. So, use these items, which good coaches use, as a guide for you and your development.

In this chapter I would like to lay out some details about what great coaches do, and that a new coach in any sport could use right away, to prepare for and run a great practice. Below you will find six categories that you can use to set up and at the end of the day analyze how effective your sessions might be with your athletes. I assert that if you frame your sessions and make sure you do well in addressing all of these things your sessions will be on target.

The 6 categories are:

1. Planning

2. Organizing

3. Environment

4. Management

5. Feedback (communication)

6. Content challenge

Again, in essence I am saying that if you do these things you are well on your way to including the 4 elements and teaching athletes content. I expand on numbers 1, 2 and 6 in the section below as they are slightly new given what we have or haven't already discussed in previous section. For 3, 4 and 5, three of the 4 elements, I provide new details but for the most part ask you to review what has already been written in previous sections.

1. Planning

How can you possibly know where you want to get to in the end if you don't plan for it at the beginning? I cannot overstate the importance of planning out your practices in detail. Setting forth, on paper, details for the practice you are about to conduct ensures accountability for all involved and ensures that you have the end in mind as you plan for that session. Having the end in mind means that by the end of the session you will have reached a certain place, so that the athlete has learned something instead of just gotten an hour older. Take the time to try some of these things as you plan your sessions:

Have a go-to lesson plan form: Be sure you have a form that you feel comfortable using to write down your session. Your sessions are basically your daily lesson plan, like a teacher. The more you can have a standard form to use the easier it is to use and the easier it will be for you to reflect on what went well and what needed work.

There are plenty of lesson plan templates for different sports online. Take time to pick around the Internet to find one that suits you as well as provides you an opportunity to include the things we are suggesting in terms of management, environment, and feedback, along with what you will be including in terms of content.

Start from the game: As you consider what you want to do for the session, relative to your topic for the day, think about how these things will transfer to the game. At the end of the day everything athletes learn should be something that fits into the game. Don't just create an activity because it looks neat and unique. Consider how that exercise may help that athlete in the game. For children, it is as simple as some technique that they will need to try in a game. Think about that before your create the exercise or drill for that day.

Have success criteria in mind: Success criteria are what you want out of the activity once you have finished. As an example, if you are doing a passing pattern for football players, is it the pattern that you care about or is it the detail within the pattern? Is it the execution of the pattern and what makes it effective that you care about? Likely the latter.

So, as you are planning step back and say, okay, when they are doing this what in the end will make this successful? Is it the speed of it, where they cut, how the ball is thrown? Start from the end in mind in terms of when they finish doing things and what makes it a successful endeavor for that time period. Have some set criteria that make it successful.

Be detailed: This one is simple: be detailed about everything in your session. Recall in a few of the sections on elements I refer to detail. This is that. Be able to answer questions like where does the activity take place on the court or field, when and for how long does the activity or progression last, how many people and which people are involved. Knowing these things ensures that everyone is involved and that there are expectations of success for all of them.

Write these things on your session for the day and work to ensure they get done. Sometimes you will deviate, yeah fine, no worries. Writing things down allows for flexibility in that you know what you want at the end of the day and, if you see something isn't working, you can make a methodical change.

Being detailed also refers to the items below, specifically how and when you will *manage, communicate* with and *challenge* the athletes. You will see below that I provide suggestions on how to do these things. Be sure to write out examples of what you might say to athletes to ensure detail, using "cues" to be certain things are done well and also serve as a remember is an example of details that you will need to include in your sessions.

__Mentally rehearse:__ Many times people write their sessions out but fail to truly work through the session that they have written. The great coaches take the time to think about what they have written and truly walk through in their minds all of that detail they have taken the time to write. Imagery is a very powerful tool for athletes to prepare for and replicate a performance prior to it actually occurring. So, too, it can be for a coach.

Remember the actor! Recall our example of the actor in our presence section — actors prepare for a performance. Actors will frequently rehearse and rehearse prior to going on stage. I would suggest the same for a coach's performance. If you, as a coach, can take the time to recall exactly what you want, when you want it and how you will communicate your thoughts, the likelihood is that when you get there you will be just that much more prepared to deliver.

2. Organized On the Day

Good coaches ensure everything is organized and ready to go at the time practice is ready to begin. In order to ensure that environment of excellence the day needs to be ready to go with details sorted out and all items in their appropriate places. Review the items below that will help you be organized on the day.

__Be on time and ready prior to players' arrival:__ It is a small thing but an important thing: be on time. Coaches who are on time show their players that it is important. As opposed to strolling in one minute after the proposed time, which says to the players that it is okay to be late, details are for other people not me. It's the wrong message and honestly sets the tone for in-game performance, because if details aren't important here, then why there?

Being on time also should be accompanied with being mentally ready. If as players arrive you are there but not mentally engaged, you're on the phone, still sorting out the day's activities, still planning on what you will be doing, that's not ready. Being mentally ready needs to accompany being on time, as it sends the message to everyone that this is practice time, switch on, and let's get after it.

Have all exercises set out and ready to go: All exercises and activities should be set out and ready to go for the day. By having everything, including all necessary equipment, ready for your sessions you can more easily teach what needs to be taught instead of worrying about what may need to be set up for your next activity.

Sometimes space is not optimal, which makes setting up every activity difficult. This happens, but it's not the athletes' fault and they deserve every opportunity to have a great learning environment. Do everything you can to ensure that the session flows from one thing to the next. Perhaps you can half set up the next space...do so. My point is do everything you can to have as many things set up as you can. After all, training sessions only last for so long and minimizing standing-around time is critical to how well you use that finite amount of time.

Ensure all equipment is in working condition: Again, a tough one sometimes, but it is critical that you check the important pieces of equipment prior to beginning your session. Items could include goals, ball machines, tackling dummies, rackets, bats. Run through a quick check of these items and ensure they are in good working condition.

3. Ensure the Environment

Okay, to the elements! As I have indicated in previous chapters, creating an environment of excellence and expectations is very important to the success of your athletes — both off the field and on. As you consider ensuring a great environment in your practice sessions be sure to keep in mind that ensuring this environment is no accident!

Recall our discussion about being a good actor? These guys and girls are not good by accident, they intend to move their audience around the place with multiple things that they say and do. You, as a master coach, should do the same as you consider creating a great environment with your people in practices. Keep in mind all of the things we talked about in the environment and try to be sure you include some of the following items from those examples.

Use that voice in your session: The voice is what often makes your session pop. Meaning, if you come out and your voice doesn't change in tone, is monotone and doesn't demand what you expect out of the day your content may or may not get taught. But if you use the tone of your voice to indicate that things must move quickly, or calm down, or people must be focused, well that's what you will get. Moreover, if you use that voice to ensure that your players understand what is expected of them, when it is expected and how quickly it is expected, stuff will get done.

Do not confuse using your voice with abusing your voice or using it out of emotion. Be smart, think about what the mood, time and topic of the session demands. Is it the right time of the session to bark or is it the right time in the session to be calm and patient? I will say, as you review some of the items I discuss in the environment section under voice hopefully they give you a sense of how and when to use that voice to ensure quality but also to ensure motivation and confidence as well as thinking skills.

Take time to review the items in the environment section and remember it is your session for player development, ensure you create that environment and also use it to teach them your content. You will have a big impact on how motivated, confident and thoughtful they are during their session just by how you use your voice to teach your content. Be mindful and use it wisely.

Be sure your body language is appropriate: Recall we talked about the importance of your body language and the signals it sends off, both to you and others. In your practice sessions be sure that you are aware of the message you want to send your players and that that message is coming out with your feedback (see below) and what you are doing with your body.

Review some of the items in the section that discuss the impact of limbs and eyes and link them with your session. Do you want players to feel comfortable making mistakes and reaching? Do you want them to understand that talking while you're talking isn't acceptable? If so, be sure that your body says that and that the players received that. At the end of the day you may be able to assess the impact your body language had on them by looking at their body language after practice. Something to consider.

Ensure focused practice: By far the biggest thing to me is ensuring a focused practice vs simply participating in the day's activity. If you look back to what I wrote on this topic in the environment section I talk about accountability and ensuring all are on task. Okay, how to do this?

The biggest way to ensure a focused practice vs simple participation is to be consistent with your demands and expectations. Don't think that you are going to go out to your session tomorrow with a group that you haven't really managed tightly and that you are going to turn them into players who are focused trainers. But doing small things, such as stopping when it isn't good enough, giving feedback relative to your high standards, freezing the group and waiting five seconds before you start talking and then communicating what changes you want and how it should be are all steps in the right direction. Starting today and keeping it going tomorrow and every other tomorrow will lead to focused training vs just showing up.

Build motivation and confidence: Not much else to say here as really if you look at the items I lay out in the environment section and try those here you will build these items within your session. I will say that you should be concrete when you are planning. That is to say, write a few exact comments that you will use to build the group or deposit items into bank accounts, relative to what you are teaching on the day. The more you do these things the more you will build these things and, as a result, a great environment where players are learning.

4. Manage the Session

As I've written a few times prior to this section, you can't manage if you can't teach. I have already written extensively about this in the management section. But it bears repeating that athletes of all ages must be managed during practices in order to ensure things are getting done.

If you flip back to the section where I reference what great coaches do to ensure players are managed during practice, you can hopefully see that all of those suggestions get us closer to ensuring players are learning and reaching expectations. There are a lot of items in this section that you can take and use right way in order to make sure items get taught (ensure listening, ensure players are focused, ensure they work to get it right, etc.). If you just took these and popped them into your session, the likelihood is that you would be teaching your content more effectively.

As I've said, the devil will always be in the details. As you look at the items I include in the management section for practice I would challenge you to be as detailed as possible about how you will handle ensuring expectations, managing focus, handling the player who isn't doing well, etc. The more detailed you are in your approach to managing your players, their effort, attention to detail and other things that are important to you, the more these things will get done. Find a few things that you feel are massively important to ensuring your message gets across and focus a lot of your management energy on those items.

5. Give Feedback

Feedback to people is critical to ensure that what you are teaching is being learned. Feedback is basically communication that manifests itself in a session. It can be verbal or nonverbal, direct or indirect, often or not so often, and is done differently with different ages, genders, levels and sports. This is where you are doing everything you can to manage the minutia of the session as well as the environment.

This is something that new coaches, and even to some extent experienced coaches, should be writing down as they plan their session. Things like, short and specific directions, cues to teach certain skills or concepts that ensure athletes get the details right, when and how often (age/level dependent) you want to give them feedback as opposed to letting them generate their own feedback are all things you could set out while you are planning your session. Other things, like which players need more gentle constructive feedback vs which ones you know you can be straightforward with; which players need more nonverbal atta-boys; and which players just need more positive communicating overall, are all things you should account for when thinking of feedback to specific types of kids.

I would also say that players should learn that they don't always need feedback. Be sure that you provide players ample opportunity to enjoy the silence and problem solve on their own. Players must be asked to think and provide their own feedback to themselves. Provide this opportunity.

At the end of the day what type, when, how and to whom you give feedback to is about timing and an understanding of what that person or moment calls for at the time. This, oddly enough, will take you a long time to get a "feel" for as you develop as a coach. Knowing the best delivery method in order to ensure learning takes experience and also being around great coaches. The more you see others do it well and then try it yourself the better you get at delivering feedback to ensure learning. Try the items I have suggested in the communication, as well as other, sections. Note what works and why it works and then refine.

6. Challenge the Athlete

Making sure your content is challenging is important if players at any level are going to stay motivated and ultimately learn to apply the skills and concepts you are working on in games or competitions. The great coach is able to set up his or her activity, get everything organized, begin the exercise, go about managing the athlete and creating a great environment by ensuring items in the exercises get taught, and then slowly begin to modify the exercise so as to challenge the athlete. These challenges come in many forms and at various times and are usually implemented to ensure stuff gets tougher, and of course all relative to the athlete's level and age!

The analogy I use to explain why challenging athletes is key is the idea of stressing the physical system out in order to develop. A system cannot grow if it is not stressed out. When athletes are looking to build physical strength do they lift the same weight over and over in order to gain muscle mass? No, they add weight, slowly and methodically, and then go about lifting that weight to gain mass; they are slowly and methodically stressing the system out.

Basically what I am getting at is if an athlete, at any level, wants to improve, there needs to be some stress that causes the athlete to change what he or she is doing in order to be successful in that activity. Recall, stress isn't always bad, some stress is actually good. If you are conducting an activity with a group of players and change how they have to play in order to be successful in that exercise, that is stress. That stress is the challenge that a coach must set forth, at the right time and just enough relative to the level of the athlete, to ensure that the athlete remains motivated and is learning the information such that they can perform it in games.

I am not suggesting tightening the screws such that the athlete freaks and loses it, but I am suggesting that the athlete must be challenged in order to be successful. There are multiple ways that different coaches do things within their sport to challenge their athletes and makes things a little more difficult so the athlete continues to grow. Below are a few suggestions that most, if not all, coaches can use in their sport to challenge their athlete.

Set limits and restrictions: Setting restrictions for athletes is an easy way to make things just a little bit more challenging within a session. Limiting things like the amount of time a player had to make a certain choice is a restriction. Another one is the space a player has to make choices in a particular activity. Another is perhaps adding a touch limit for certain sports, like soccer or basketball, which can ensure players are forced to make different choices in what is likely less time given the less touches rule. Each of these examples, when manipulated at the right time, ensures that the activity becomes a bit more challenging.

Another example to make activities more challenging is increasing or decreasing the number of players involved in the activity. Depending on the activity, this modification requires the athlete to solve more or less problems. Things like adding more goals, balls or movement after a choice, can also add to the complexity of the decision-making process.

Whatever is done the timing of it is obviously key. Adding too many problems too early may send that player or group in the wrong direction. Be sure to try small things slowly to make things more challenging for the athlete.

Challenge the athlete: I mention this in the section on fostering thinking, because asking questions to athletes instead of constantly giving them the answers is challenge the athlete to *think*. This is important by itself. But make it challenging for everyone by ensuring that you ask the question without putting a name on it.

In a group of 23 players if you ask the question "What are some of the ways we can do such and such?" This is good. You have left it for the entire group by not saying, "Billy…" and then the question. This says you are talking to Billy and that everyone else can tune out because they didn't hear their name. You should make sure you have an answer in mind and you are not fishing without knowing the answer. It shouldn't be guess work on your part, too, as they are trying to put your puzzle together, not make their own puzzle!

Make it competitive: Competition is good. No matter what the age or level, ensuring competition in order to challenge the athlete is good and necessary. The key is knowing how and when to do it given the level and abilities of your athletes.

Asking young players to compete is also a good thing. What we need to define is what is meant by competition. Challenging players to focus for greater periods of time is a competition, challenging a young player to improve on a skill relative to how he or she did it last time is a competition, asking players to compete against a specific time or other fixed quantity is also fine. These are all good things to do to ensure kids are challenged as we are asking them to compete on things that they have control over. Also important here is how we have set up our environment for them to handle the competition. Are they successful when they work hard or do they have to win all the time or be perfect? Use this as a time to challenge the young athlete to compete against himself or herself and to learn to see that they are successful as they try things.

Having older athletes compete is absolutely essential to ensuring a challenging environment. Including competitions within an athlete and between athletes is very important to an athlete's development. Some athletes do not like to compete and this just cannot be. Athletes need to understand that competition can be a very healthy thing if they understand that the goal is to make sure they get better vs to judge them vs another person. Providing athletes with opportunities to compete in trainings in small games, individual activities and large group games is a great way to challenge them in order that they stay motivated and engaged in the session.

Review progress often: Reviewing what the players have learned in the session provides them concrete evidence that they have progressed. This shows that they have accepted previous challenges and that they have reached the expectations and demands that you have laid down. This is making a direct deposit into that bank of success. This is a good time to follow up with a comment like "don't be satisfied;" and then seeing what else they can do relative to what they just did.

Challenge at the right time: Sometimes athletes need to be pushed and sometimes they need to be pulled. Meaning there may be times that you must spot that moment (or moments) when an athlete needs that next challenge in training — continue to challenge him or her and demand that he or she continue after it in different ways until they progress. But, sometimes the last thing an athlete needs is more challenge or tweaks, as they haven't mastered what you've given them and they are frustrated. At this time it is more of a pulling them along thing by helping them with what is in front of them. Provide that encouragement, and when they are ready, then it's on to the next challenge.

Being an effective coach and teacher of content takes time and concentrated effort to master. The best coaches use the ideas set forth within the 4 elements to make sure their practices are fruitful every time they step on the court or field. They also take time to plan and organize their sessions down to every detail. Taking this time and careful approach to coaching ensures that players learn the content that you are setting out to teach. Being a great coach takes time, but the benefits are apparent once you seen those well-prepared teams and athletes play.

Also, as you watch great coaches, understand that they know their content very well and that they have an ability to teach that content just as well as any classroom teacher teaches his or her subject. The great coach understands that he or she is never perfect but approaches his or her craft with a daily pursuit of being great with the goal of helping their players learn to play the game better as a result of that session. This isn't a sometimes thing; it's an all-the-time thing.

Getting good at these things take a great deal of time to get right but also a great deal of methodical work to begin to be great at the content as well as innovative ways to teach that content. Great coaches take that time to be detailed in their sessions, from the planning and organization to the management of their players, and from the environment they create to the feedback they give their players. These things are detailed and purposeful. This purposeful approach isn't accomplished overnight and it isn't developed by some innate genius, it's built.

For those who are embarking on a coaching career, I strongly suggest getting as much information on various content and teaching methodologies relative to your sport that you can get your hands on. Sessions and pedagogical methods are readily available in books or online but, getting into licensing programs and being around great coaches who use these things is really the best way to go. Putting yourself in these positions to gain experience and learn from these experiences is what separates good coaches from great coaches.

Chapter 9

Gaining Experience
and Experiences

A twenty-five-year-old with two years of coaching experience and a fifty-five-year-old with 32 years of coaching experience are coaching the exact same exercise — what is the difference? Well, assuming you could make an astute educated judgment (perhaps even based on our criteria from the previous section), and they were both of quality, the differences would be astounding. You would likely see the experienced coach doing all sorts of small nuanced things as he or she taught the players the content in the session. The young coach would probably have a few items in the 4 elements down and even look the part — but the details and subtleties that the veteran coach displayed, assuming they were of quality of course, would be just tastier to watch.

Watching a great coach work with people who happen to be athletes is as beautiful as watching any masterpiece take shape. The things that they do, say, coerce, move around and try with their athletes in order to teach is like a conductor conducting an orchestra. They understand where the music needs to go, what instruments need to do what and when, they allow the different musicians to come in and be loud when they need to and bring it all together at the right time so as to make something truly amazing. The experienced conductor allows freedom and flexibility to the musicians within the musical score and ensures he or she is firm or loose when the rhythm of the music calls for such things. It is truly art and science that is making this sensational music and takes years to master.

Gaining experience as a coach who is putting the person first takes real time, effort and experience and allows that great coach to just see things differently. Experienced coaches can see different things that need addressing with the person because they have seen it before. The game has slowed down for them much like it does for an athlete who has played for fifteen years as a pro. In sessions, experienced coaches are able to see multiple things almost before they are happening and make adjustments, suggestions, or twists and turns in the session as needed, whereas a novice coach only sees and can adjust one or two things at a time. The fantastic thing about veteran coaches is that when they do it, it looks effortless.

But how do coaches get to this place? What are the things that they did to gain experience? And are experiences different than experience? Before answering these questions, let's get a working picture of that coach who oozes experience(s): Coach K of Duke basketball.

Mike Krzyzewski is a fantastically successful basketball coach with massive amounts of coaching experience and what appear to be unique life experiences. Coach Krzyzewski, also known as Coach K, is the Duke men's basketball coach. He is one of the most successful basketball coaches of all time and is revered among both his peers and leaders of industry. Coach K has been the coach of college teams that have been to eleven "Final Fours" and that have won four NCAA basketball championships. He has also been the head coach for the USA Men's basketball team, with teams that won the Gold medal in the Beijing and London Olympics in 2008 and 2012, respectively. He is also a highly sought-after speaker on leadership and what it takes to compete at an elite level. He is truly a master coach who took years to develop. Coach K has experience. To write about his resume in just a few sentences is to do it an injustice. Suffice it to say that he has an extensive coaching resume.

More importantly, though, he has a resume that includes high-level coaching experiences with incredible coaches and athletes.

Coach K has coached basketball since 1974 and has coached under and alongside true legends of the game. At Army, where Coach K started coaching, he coached under Bob Knight, one of the true legends of the game. In the 1984 Olympics, he assisted Coach Knight with the Olympic team that won Gold in Los Angeles. Coach K returned to assist the Olympic team in 1992. This team was no ordinary team, this was the Dream Team with players like Michael Jordan, Magic Johnson, Larry Bird and more! In addition, the team was coached by some true legends as well in Chuck Daly, Lenny Wilkens, and P.J. Carlisimo. If you don't know these names or resumes, they were true giants of the game. Needless to say this type of experience is invaluable and no doubt contributed to his success as he came back to successfully lead his university and country to glory. But sport experience is not the only experience one needs to be great; after all we coach people, we don't coach athletes.

Coach K appeared to understand from the beginning that sports were about people and relationships and, as a result, sought out experiences that lent themselves to improving him as a person and as a coach. My favorite stories about Coach K are the ones from off the court. Coach K has spoken many times about the impact that his family life has had on him as a person and a coach. He credits his family with imparting religious values and instilling a drive to work hard, just as they had done as first generation Americans from Poland. He also credits his family life as a husband and parent as assisting him in developing some of his most important tenets as a coach.

Much has been written about how Coach K was influenced by the women in his life. Coach K is married and has three daughters. It was said that he observed that the girls were extremely communicative and very astute about what was going on with people, what they were feeling and what they might be thinking. In fact it has been said that one of his daughters would frequently point out when Coach K's players were upset about something, and in most cases she was right about what she saw in that athlete. Coach K would apparently take note of the way in which the girls would operate and go about their day watching and communicating with people, including him. Eventually this seems to have impacted his coaching as it has been said that his relationships and cultivating those relationships are critical to how he coaches his athletes. This has become a cornerstone to Coach K's philosophy and, as a result, has likely helped him develop hundreds of athletes and win multiple championships at different levels.

Coach K got experience and learned from his experiences, and so can you. It is imperative for any coach that he or she gain actual experience coaching, at various levels and ages. There is an oft-used number of hours of experience that one must arrive at before one becomes great; this number is 10,000 hours. This number has been used in multiple publications and has its roots in research. But it is an arbitrary number, as the number of hours one amasses are only as good as the experiences that occur over those hours and the effort one puts into those hours and experiences. Coach K, and other great coaches, not only put themselves into positions to get experience as they coach with great coaches but also put very thought-filled efforts to learn every time, and hour, they engage in those coaching experiences. These coaching experiences add up and over the hours of time develop the person in each of the 4 elements and beyond.

I would also argue that of equal importance to coaching experience are life experiences and learning from those experiences. I can't tell you the number of times I have learned something by watching a good teacher, watching a good TV character, listening to a radio icon interview somebody, having a drink with a friend or simply by watching how other people handle stuff. There is literally an opportunity to learn everywhere and at any time. The key to learning from life's experiences is to be aware and put the experiences in context.

Everybody has life experiences but the emerging great coach puts himself or herself into meaningful situations and frames what they are watching in order to help them be great. Emerging great coaches put themselves with great coaches and great teachers. They take the time to attend sessions, get licensed and educated, and be around as many of these educational opportunities as possible. They also then take what they see, make meaning of it based on things in the 4 elements and relative to their sport, write it down and try it out. I cannot stress the importance of this step, that is, deriving meaning from an experience; gaining from experiences is critical and a must-have part of a coach's development. This idea of putting it in your context or framing your experience takes real effort, but the opportunities to do this are endless.

Coaching is more than learning to coach, it is learning how to work with and improve people, and the experiences to help you get great at this are everywhere. Take a peek at the items below regarding getting experience and experiences. In no way is this an exhaustive list but, as above, I would argue that if you can do this over 5, 10, 15 years, the likelihood is that you will be pretty solid at your craft.

15 steps to experience

1. Take Notes

You are going to see a lot of stuff as you collect experiences. If you do not write stuff down there is a good chance that you will either forget what you experience, or at best, not recall the details of how it went, how it made you feel and, of course, how it impacted people around that experience.

Personally, I have a terrible memory and I know this. As a result I write everything down, sessions, ideas, things I see or go through. When I first started writing stuff down, computers weren't used that much (yes, I'm old) so I would write on scraps of paper. Then, slowly I began to take notes on computer and file things away, on a floppy disc! Over time, and even now, I use my phone, email, whatever I can to jot things down. I strongly suggest that as you look at the items below and generate your places/times/people to gather experiences with and, from that, you write it down and create a very organized filing system; I assure you it's worth it.

2. Develop Self-Awareness

Hopefully you'll notice that the first two things that I put down have nothing to do with what to see or do but more about how to see them. I spoke about building self-awareness previously but as you gain experiences it is important that you learn to be self-aware relative to those experiences.

Be self-aware of how they make you feel, think and, of course, whether or not this is something you have or even want in your repertoire. Sometimes you will have an experiences that makes you say, "Yikes, that was awful, I don't ever want to be like that!" Good, that's a great experience; sometimes we learn about who we want to be and what we want to do by experiencing the complete opposite. Other times you will experience things that are fantastic and amazing and leave you saying

"I want to be like that!" Again, great but don't get caught up in the emotion, pay attention to what they did, how they did it and how it made you and others feel.

This is so important! Be aware of what is going on at that time and really learn from it. I say this to my kids all the time, take the moment to be in the moment as it's the last moment like that moment that you'll ever have. And it's true, real life stuff can't be repeated. Be aware of what is going on and write it down, and for goodness' sake, be in the moment.

3. Coach

Simple enough, no? In order to be a great coach you need to get out and coach. Talk about getting 10,000 hours, this is built hour-by-hour and session-by-session. Take any opportunity to get out and coach, but be present every time.

Recall I said hours aren't worth a salt if you are not getting something out of those hours. Don't just show up, that doesn't give you any experience. Go out and run the best session that you can, every time, and you will fall short frequently but this is a good thing. It is certainly better than just showing up and rolling a ball and saying, "Okay, kids go get it." This does nothing for anyone. Get out there and coach, make it fun, make it exciting coach a little or coach a lot, but do it purposefully!

Also, be sure to get some coaching experience with different ages, genders and abilities. Getting these different experiences provides you with a different vantage point on the same sport. This different vantage point expands the number of scenarios you will see and ultimately lead you to being a better coach because you will have seen more things. I have seen this firsthand with a number of my colleagues who are coaching professionally or collegiately. They have coached these different ages and levels and genders and, because of these experiences, they have unique ways of dealing with issues that pop up in their new situation.

4. Get Educated In Your Sport

Find time to attend licenses, seminars, workshops and other educational opportunities within your sport. Most sports have governing bodies or entities that organize these opportunities. A lot of them are actually pretty solid in how they provide the basics for the sport. Some of these entities actually grant coaching licenses that move you along a continuum in terms of your "level" as a coach. Again, some of these are good and some are average, but they are all opportunities to improve.

Sometimes attending these things gives more than just educational opportunities — they provide opportunities to network, be social and hoop-jump. Networking and being social is part of getting educated in your sport. These workshops usually involve overnight stays, lunches, etc., and these are good times to really get a good sense of the material covered as well as get to know other like-minded folks who share the same fashion. By "hoop-jump" I mean that being educated is important but it is also just as important that others know you are getting educated. When your athletes understand that you are putting time into getting educated, it says to them that improving is important to all of us, including me.

No matter what, make time to get educated in your sport. It'll make a big difference over time and shows that you are serious about your craft.

5. Get Educated Outside of Your Sport

Being educated outside of sport is also important because it adds to your knowledge repertoire. Taking classes at university, in person or online, not only moves you close to a degree but it makes you a better coach. I remember when I first started coaching, I knew I lacked that high-level playing experience that would be needed if I wanted to be that next-level coach at the college or pro level. So, I supplemented. I ensured I had a background that was as unique as anybody's and could contribute to the success of an athlete or coaching staff.

Going to school in order to earn a degree is not the goal. Find a school and a program that improves you as a person and also lends itself to helping you be a better coach. There aren't many universities with coaching degrees, so what. Make your degree what you want it to be. I would strongly encourage those of you who want to be a great coach to find a school that offers the opportunity to get better at improving people in a performance setting. Perhaps it's a teaching program, a therapy program, a communication program. It doesn't matter; put whatever you learn in your context. Take what you learn that day, week or month and go out and practice. That is what education is for, to make an impact on you so that you can make an impact on others.

6. Watch and Be Around Great Coaches

I cannot stress the importance of this in a person's development. For me personally I have done all of the coaching licenses, attended workshops and gone to plenty of schools, but the place where I improved the most was at other coaches' sessions. When you are around great coaches, you see the way sessions are supposed to be conducted. You can see the elements, content, and various teaching methodologies at work. The biggest thing here is that you need to take time to see what you are seeing.

Taking time to see what you are seeing means step back and take it all in. When you watch great coaches coach you may take for granted how smooth the session is running and not really take time to ask yourself, "Why is it moving along without any glitches?" I'll tell you why, they are managing their session, communicating effectively and ensuring a great environment — and this takes real work. Take a step back, and really watch those little things that I have said good coaches do relative to those 4 elements, and you will see them.

7. Watch Other Coaches In Other Sports

Taking time to watch good coaches in other sports can give you a fresh look on the same problem. Kids in basketball have to defend, as do kids in football, hockey, lacrosse and other sports. Watching other coaches move their players around, literally and figuratively, can provide you with some different perspectives that perhaps you haven't thought of because many coaches within the same sport have been "doing it this way for years." Take time to do the things described above when watching a good coach, but tweak the way you internalize it.

8. Watch Good Teachers

I can without a doubt say that this one made a profound impact on me as a teacher and coach. I have been around methodical, caring teachers in my time. The number of things I have used from their daily classroom sessions are just too many to count.

Spending time around good teachers, both in and out of the classroom, will provide you real-life examples of every single one of the items I have mentioned in this book. For me, a good teacher is a good coach and vice-versa. School is just another performance setting, so watching how these folks prepare for, engage in, chat about and ultimately deliver their content to their students as they prepare them for life (and of course tests and quizzes) is as good as it gets. Plop yourself down in a kindergarten class that is run by an expert sometime. You will see some serious management of an environment through communication; it's awesome. Take any opportunity you have to watch the good ones as it is a real eye-opener.

9. Be Mentored

If you are lucky enough you can find someone who cares enough to (and is good enough to) mentor you as you develop. Mentors provide that trustworthy information source that not only gives you examples of stuff to do but also gives you a chance to bounce stuff off of them as you develop. The good ones are not only good coaches but good people and can really give you feedback about how you are progressing relative to getting there yourself.

Choose wisely! As you go about working with someone and you think, okay, this person could be a good mentor, they very well may be.

But, then again, they may not. Keep your eyes wide open — watch how that person treats people and manages himself or herself when no one is watching as that is who that person really is.

Sometimes a mentor isn't a mentor but rather an example of how to do certain things and not do things. I have been around people who I thought were good mentors, and for a while they were, until it didn't serve their purpose anymore, or I saw them do things that were just completely self-serving. These people are out there, just be aware and take what you like from what they do and leave the rest alone; no one is perfect and that's okay, too.

I tell you what though, if you can find that good one who is more altruistic than not, you are flying. I have had the good fortune of having one or two of these in my life as well, they are game changers. Are they a good person? Do they help you learn life lessons? Do they treat you like a person? That's a mentor!

10. Be a Mentor

When you develop into a great coach, now it's your turn. Talk about a good experience, helping move someone down a path is very rewarding. As I said, I have had some fantastically caring teachers who mentored me as a teacher and coach, when I am not sure I deserved that kind of attention and assistance. As a result, though, I had some wonderful examples when it was my turn.

I think it is an incredible learning experience to be a mentor. You are forced to look inward often and really check yourself to see if what you are doing and saying is helping that person develop. The place that I always start with is, am I doing everything I can to prepare this person to be in front of one of my sons in the classroom or on the field? If I am, then I am doing it right; if I am not, then that's no good. Opening myself up to that kind of feeling has allowed me to get the most out of assisting someone in moving along their coaching continuum, as if I do a bad job and they are in front of one of my sons then it's my fault, and that is never going to happen!

As you take on this role, remember, it is not about you. These people trust you and what you are saying and doing with them. Recall previously I said once someone trusts you, you can get away with a lot, and that is a big responsibility. This responsibility is something you must understand and hold in high regard when you take on this role. Again, I have had some people I thought were mentors but in the end they were simply interested in their development and well-being, which I have sadly seen play out as they have aged. Make sure you always keep in mind that this person trusts you and that it is about their development, not yours. This is a tough place to get to (and one I am continuing to try to be aware of for me on a daily basis), but good for self-reflection and ultimately for a growth experience for both parties.

At the end of the day these experiences — both in being mentored and mentoring; both done well and poorly — will help in building experiences and contributing to your development as a coach. I would suggest that you take on each of these roles (mentor and mentee) over the years to help you become better as a coach and person. Take on each of these roles with self-awareness and humility and a desire to make a difference in athletes' lives as a result of both.

11. Watch People In Different Performance Settings

Have you ever watched a good waiter in a busy restaurant? They are taking orders, inputting orders, delivering food, talking with customers, listening to bosses, chefs and others, all while maintaining calm and focus on ensuring their job get done, over and over. These guys and girls are good. They have presence, create a great environment at their tables, by managing their customers and orders through communication; it's as good as it gets!

Take time to watch anyone in a performance setting. Honestly, plop yourself down and just watch people in performance settings where they are working with people. There are all sorts of opportunities to watch people who are working with other people who need to be moved along a continuum. Watch what those people do well and poorly and how they handle both outcomes.

12. Read

Read about lots of people. Read books about good coaches, great leaders, and former great leaders and unique people. Read books on different disciplines, read books on how business have developed and failed; read articles on all kinds of subjects. Read.

I strongly suggest that you take the time to read many types of things and frame them from a perspective of the 4 elements and/or coaching perspective. You should always be asking yourself, "What can I take from this and where can this improve me as a person and a coach?" I think the more types of things you read the more worldly it makes you and the more it opens your mind. Once your mind is open, and you are looking at it in context, you can take what you need from what you read.

13. Talk About Stuff With Like-Minded People

If you like a glass of wine or beer or a cup of coffee, this is an easy one. Once you have done, watched, and read about coaching stuff, talk about it. Those nights where you are shooting the breeze about what this coach did well, what you liked about this person's session, what you liked that that world leader said, can almost always come back to your session or sport and how what they did would also be great if it was done similarly with your players.

Be sure you listen as well. Sometimes when we get together with colleagues we want to share our ideas and experiences. Not a problem, but also be sure that you are listening as well as they could have had a similar experience that could reshape your experience, and lead to real growth for you (and your players).

These times are almost always when come crazy good ideas are tossed out and started. This is your "Google time" to be creative. You know stuff, other people know stuff, share and pick apart all that stuff with the goal of just talking about stuff related to good coaching! It's heaven.

14. Assess Yourself

Take time to assess yourself via video or a handwritten assessment. I mention videoing previously but in this case taking time to assess yourself means that you are maximizing the impact of your experience because you are being critical of that experience. Be fair to yourself, though, and ensure you are not all over the place when you assess yourself.

Take the items in the "teaching content" area and create a handwritten assessment tool to rate yourself on, for example, 15 things that you would like to see yourself do well. This written assessment can have a rating system from 1 to 5, and as you spot these things on the video, make notes of each of them and use this same sheet a week, a month, a year later to see how you have progressed.

I use these assessment tools all the time to assess coaches as they develop. I use a 1 to 5 rating system and keep the evaluations as we work to improve over time. They are wonderful tools and really show how far a coach has come over time as he or she gets more and more experience.

15. Build and Deliver Your Ethics

Being a coach means having sound ethics. Do you know what is important to you? Do you know why? Is this apparent in your philosophy? Your sessions? Your meetings with players or families?

Building and checking your ethics takes real introspective thought and an awareness of how you behave all the time. It is imperative that you have a strong sense of what is right relative to your philosophy and that that is getting across to your athletes often. Players can spot a coach who isn't ethical: saying one thing but doing another, wishy-washy with rules, etc. Take time to see if the way you are behaving jives with your rules and what you are telling players is important to you and your program.

Epilogue

Hopefully as you have read this book you have picked up some little gems that you have already used with your athletes. For me the goal is always to provide anybody working with an individual in a performance setting with ideas and examples that will enhance how they develop that performer as a person first. While I understand this is a long journey filled with many uncertainties I also realize the more you know the more you can be a part of developing people in any sport and at any level you coach.

Presence, Environment, Management, Communication and Experience take years and years to develop. But these elements and characteristics don't develop by accident. These things take a concentrated, focused effort to spot in others, to practice as yours, and to be great at — in time — for others. This is truly a fantastic journey and one that I hope you are encouraged to take.

I hope our relationship does not end here. I am passionate about positively impacting people in any performance setting. I think I have learned from some sensational teachers and feel obligated and excited to continue to pass it on. Please connect with me at DrLeeHancock.com.

Footnotes

1. Ibrahimovic, Zlatan. (2013) *I am Zlatan*. New York, New York: Random House Trade Paperbacks.

2. Hawkey, Ian. (2014, February 24). "Didier Drogba faces test of emotions in special reunion when he takes on Chelsea and Jose Mourinho" [online article]. Retrieved from http://www.telegraph.co.uk/sport/football/teams/chelsea/10659442/Didier-Drogba-faces-test-of-emotions-in-special-reunion-when-he-takes-on-Chelsea-and-Jose-Mourinho.html

3. Youngmisuk, Ohm. (2014, March 17). "Michael Jordan: Phil can do it" [online article]. Retrieved from http://espn.go.com/new-york/nba/story/_/id/10624224/michael-jordan-believes-phil-jackson-turn-new-york-knicks

4. Ferguson, Sir Alex. (2013) *Alex Ferguson: My Autobiography*. London, England: Hodder & Stoughton.

5. Scott. (2013, September 12). "Ferguson: I had to chase Becks, Scholes and Giggs in from training" [online article]. Retrieved from http://therepublikofmancunia.com/ferguson-i-had-to-chase-becks-scholes-and-giggs-in-from-training/

6. Wooden, John. [online diagram] Retrieved from http://tobefree.files.wordpress.com/2010/06/john-woodens-pyramid-of-success.jpg

7. Brennan, Eamonn. (2010, June 5). "Bill Walton remembers his friend, coach" [online article]. Retrieved from http://espn.go.com/blog/collegebasketballnation/tag/_/name/john-wooden-2010

8. Dr. Derek Cabrera. (2011, December 6). Dr. Derek Cabrera - How Thinking Works. Retrieved from https://www.youtube.com/watch?v=dUqRTWCdXt4&noredirect=1

9. *The Wall Street Journal*. (2014). "What do Managers do?" [online article]. Retrieved from http://guides.wsj.com/management/developing-a-leadership-style/what-do-managers-do/

10. Anderson, Lars. (2014, July 21). "NICK SABAN AND THE PROCESS" [online article]. Retrieved from http://www.sportsonearth.com/article/85531726/the-process-nick-saban-university-of-alabama-crimson-tide

Notes

Notes

Notes

Notes